barefoot knits

one yarn...one pair of needles...endless possibilities

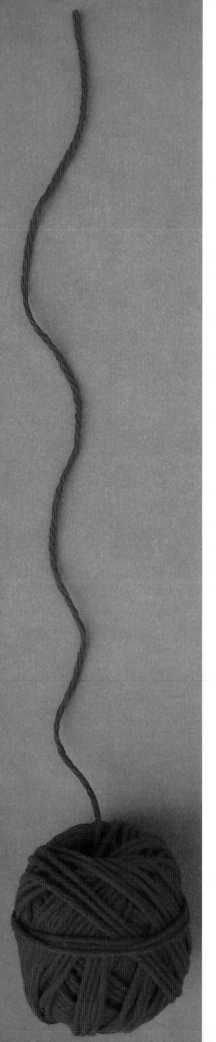

First published in the United States of America in 2005 by
Christine Schwender and Paula Heist
Memphis, Tennessee 38139

Text and photographs ©
Christine Schwender and Paula Heist 2005

ISBN 0-9769697-0-X

Printed and bound in the United States by Toof Press

table of contents

introduction

one yarn

We began our pattern writing and knitting using Brown Sheep Cotton Fleece with the intention of using other yarns throughout the book. Then the inevitable happened...we became addicted. It was inexpensive to knit, our children could actually wear it, and believe it or not - we could throw it in the washer and dryer. Christine begs to differ with Paula's opinion on the dryer but grudgingly, will admit that drying these garments inside out works (refer to the yarn label for the actual washing instructions provided by Brown Sheep Company). Cotton Fleece is easily available in many yarn stores, in a wide range of colors.

one pair of needles

Every pattern in this book is knit with a pair of size US 6 14" straight needles to make life easy.

endless possibilities

All of our designs can be knit in any color combination imaginable.
Customize it to fit your personality.
Make it your own.

knit down dress, 52

6

raglan dress, 54

knit down sweater, 66

tank top, 68   ruffle skirt, 72   ruffle pant, 70

13

baby blanket, 74

lace-up cardigan, 76

long skirt, 80

rugby
sweater, 82

three tier skirt, 86

spiral skirt, 88

back pack, 90

tic tac toe pouch, 92

halter top, 94

short shorts, 58

tube top, 104
halter top, 94

24

halter dress, 96

lace-up
poncho, 98

tank dress, 100

vest, 102

tube top, 104

wrap dress, 106

heart purse, 110

triangle purse, 112

leftover throw, 114

seed dress, 116˝

raglan sweater, 120

capris, 122

long skirt, 80

long skirt, 80

color block
poncho, 124

43

gift bag, 126

heart and flower pillows 127

capris, 122

halter dress, 96

tank dress, 100

endless
possibilities

general information

Always read a pattern through to the end before beginning. Plan and map out your knitting journey. Know what you are going to do at each row (refer to example on page 101). Doing this gives you freedom to adjust length or use different colors of yarn.

Each pattern lists actual measurements of the garment, not the child.

knitting essentials

So what should every knitter carry around? First and foremost, it is important to purchase a knitting bag that you love, or for that matter, knit one. Next, find a zipper pouch with a clear plastic front (the kind we all had in grade school to hold our pens, pencils, crayons and sharpeners). You will easily be able to identify the contents and find what you are looking for. Once you have these two items, you are ready to start purchasing the tools of the trade.

- Pair of size US 6 14" knitting needles - invest in a great pair (we recommend Lantern Moon hardwood needles - see resources)
- Scissors
- Tapestry needle
- Tape measure (retractable soft tape)
- Stitch holders
- Pair of size 6 double-pointed needles
- Crochet hook
- Safety pin
- Nail file - this is not for when your manicure has seen better days. The occasional spliced, chipped or frayed nail will seriously interfere with your knitting.

yarn

Yarn amounts provided in the patterns are based on the amounts used by the person who knit the garment. Slight variations will occur when considering the differences in gauge. When purchasing yarn, always check that the dye lot numbers provided on the labels are the same.

gauge

Before beginning a project, knit a swatch to measure your gauge. A tighter or looser gauge will have an effect on the finished size of the garment. To knit a swatch, cast on 25 stitches and continue in stockinette stitch until piece measures 5" from cast on edge. Measure your stitches by placing a ruler horizontally on the piece. Count the stitches between four inches. Place the ruler vertically on the piece and count the number of rows between four inches. The gauge for all patterns in this book is 20 stitches and 28 rows to 4" square measured over stockinette stitch using US 6 needles. If you have more stitches, your gauge is tight and you may need to work with larger needles. If you have less stitches, your gauge is loose and you should try smaller needles.

Remember, one yarn, one pair of needles, means one swatch to knit.

abbreviations

dec	decrease
inc	increase
k	knit
m1ls	make one left slant (see notes below)
m1rs	make one right slant (see notes below)
p	purl
rs	right side
skp	slip 1, knit 1, pass slipped stitch over knit stitch (decreases one stitch)
st	stitch
sts	stitches
st st	stockinette stitch
tog	together
ws	wrong side
yo	yarn over

notes   make one left slant: this is an increase technique that makes a stitch in between two existing stitches. To work this increase, insert the left needle from the front to back under the horizontal 'ladder' between the two needles. Knit this lifted strand through the back to twist the stitch to the left.

make one right slant: to work this increase, insert the left needle from the back to front under the horizontal 'ladder' between two stitches. Knit this lifted strand through the front to twist the stitch to the right. Refer to *The Knitter's Companion* (see resources)

i-cord

Using double-pointed needles, cast on 4 stitches. Knit all stitches. Switch needles so that the needle with the stitches is in your left hand. Slide stitches to other end of needle and knit this row. Continue switching needles, sliding yarn and knitting stitches until the desired length is reached.

tie-dying

It is quite simple to transform a knitted garment into a tie-dyed masterpiece. We tie-dyed the halter top, tube top, and long skirt using permanent dye. Here is where your creativity can reign. Make horizontal or vertical stripes, circles of various sizes, even try dipping the garment in two different dyes. We used Dylon® Permanent Fabric Dye. Don't forget to wrap the rubberbands tightly to ensure that you have clearly defined white areas.   Proceed with the dying instructions provided by the manufacturer on the label (see resources).

Notice the reactions you will get to the unique qualities of a tie-dyed knitted piece. People often wonder if a zebra is black with white stripes or white with black stripes. Now people have something else to wonder about - did you knit in Caribbean Sea and bleach it, or knit in Cotton Ball and dye it? By the way, a zebra is really white with black stripes (a special thanks to the docent at the Memphis Zoo for confirming this information). Like zebras, no two tie-dyed pieces will ever be the same. The possibilities truly are endless.

knit down dress

The simplicity of this dress, the elegance of the slight hip shaping and the side slits make it a 'must knit'. This dress begins at the neck and upper sleeve edge and is knit to the hem.

materials	1 (2, 2, 2, 3) ball(s) Brown Sheep Cotton Fleece in Buttercream (A)
	2 (3, 3, 3, 4) balls Brown Sheep Cotton Fleece in Provincial Rose (B)
	Pair of size US 6 14" knitting needles
gauge	20 sts and 28 rows = 4" square measured over st st using US 6 needles
size	2 (4, 6, 8, 10)
finished measurements	Armspan: 35 ½ (38, 41, 45, 49)"
	Chest: 20 (22, 24, 26, 28)"
	Length from cast on edge to hem: 22 (24, 26, 28, 30)"
front & back alike	Cast on 178 (191, 204, 225, 246) sts with A.

Row 1: k.
Row 2: p76 (82, 88, 97, 106), k26 (27, 28, 31, 34), p76 (82, 88, 97, 106).
Repeat rows 1 and 2 one more time.
Beginning with a k row, continue in st st until piece measures 3 (3 ½, 3 ½, 4, 4 ½)" from cast on edge ending with a p row.
At the beginning of next eight rows: cast off 16 (17, 18, 20, 22) sts. There are now 50 (55, 60, 65, 70) sts remaining.
Next row (rs): join in B, beginning with a k row, continue in st st until piece measures 10 ½ (11 ½, 12 ½, 13 ½, 14 ½)" from cast on edge ending with a p row.
Next row (inc row): k2, m1rs, k to last 2 sts, m1ls, k2.
Beginning with a p row, continue in st st increasing two sts (as in inc row) every 4th (6th, 8th, 10th, 12th) row until there are 58 (63, 68, 73, 78) sts.
Continue in st st until piece measures 19 (20, 22, 23, 25)" from cast on edge ending with a p row.
Next row: k.
Next row: k4, p to last 4 sts, k4.
Repeat last two rows two more times.
Next row (rs): cast off 1 st, k to end.
Next row (ws): cast off 1 st, k2, p to last 3 sts, k3.
Next row: k.
Next row: k3, p to last 3 sts, k3.
Repeat last two rows until piece measures 21 ½ (23 ½, 25 ½, 27 ½, 29 ½)" from cast on edge ending with a ws row.
K five rows.
Cast off.

finishing	Join shoulder, sleeve and side seams.

raglan dress

materials	2 (3, 3, 4, 4) balls Brown Sheep Cotton Fleece in Wolverine Blue (A) 1 ball Brown Sheep Cotton Fleece in Putty (B) Pair of size US 6 14" knitting needles 3 buttons
gauge	20 sts and 28 rows = 4" square measured over st st using US 6 needles
size	2 (4, 6, 8, 10)
finished measurements	Chest: 22 ½ (24, 26 ½, 29 ½, 32)" Length: 19 (24, 29 ½, 32, 34)"

front

Cast on 74 (80, 86, 92, 98) sts with A.
K six rows.
Next row (dec row): k2, skp, k to last 4 sts, k2tog, k2.
Beginning with a p row, continue in st st decreasing 2 sts (as in dec row) every 8th (10th, 14th, 16th, 18th) row until there are 56 (60, 66, 74, 80) sts remaining ending with a p row. Continue in st st until piece measures 14 (18 ½, 23 ½, 25, 26 ½)" from cast on edge ending with a p row.

Armhole shaping:
Next row (rs): cast off 6 sts, k to end.
Next row (ws): cast off 6 sts, p to end.
There are now 44 (48, 54, 62, 68) sts remaining.
Next row: k3, skp, k to last 5 sts, k2tog, k3.
Next row: p.
Repeat last two rows until there are 20 (22, 24, 26, 28) sts remaining ending with a p row. Place sts on holder.

back

Cast on 74 (80, 86, 92, 98) sts with A.
K six rows.
Next row (dec row): k2, skp, k to last 4 sts, k2tog, k2.
Beginning with a p row, continue in st st decreasing 2 sts (as in dec row) every 8th (10th, 14th, 16th, 18th) row until there are 56 (60, 66, 74, 80) sts remaining ending with a p row. Continue in st st until piece measures 14 (18 ½, 23 ½, 25, 26 ½)" from cast on edge ending with a p row.

Armhole shaping:
Next row (rs): cast off 6 sts, k to end.
Next row (ws): cast off 6 sts, p to end.
There are now 44 (48, 54, 62, 68) sts remaining.

Divide for back placket opening (right side):
Next row (rs): k3, skp, k15 (17, 20, 24, 27), place safety pin through next 4 sts on left hand needle, k these 4 sts (see notes below). Turn and work on these 23 (25, 28, 32, 35) sts only.

Next row (ws): k4, p to end.
Row 1 (rs): k3, skp, k to end.
Row 2: k4, p to end.
Repeat rows 1 and 2, 2 (2, 3, 4, 5) more times.
Next row (button hole): k3, skp, k to last 3 sts, yo, k2tog, k1.
Next row (ws): k4, p to end.
Repeat rows 1 and 2 above 3 (4, 4, 5, 6) more times.
Next row (button hole): k3, skp, k to last 3 sts, yo, k2tog, k1.
Next row (ws): k4, p to end.
Repeat rows 1 and 2 above until there are 12 (13, 14, 15, 16) sts remaining. Place sts on holder.

Left side placket:
Place 4 sts from safety pin on to left hand needle, rejoin yarn, k to last 5 sts, k2tog, k3.
Next row (ws): p to last 4 sts, k4.
Next row (rs): k to last 5 sts, k2tog, k3.
Repeat last two rows until there are 12 (13, 14, 15, 16) sts remaining.
Next row: p to last 4, sts k4. Place sts on holder.

sleeves
make 2 alike
Cast on 44 (47, 52, 59, 64) sts with B.
K six rows.
Beginning with a p row, continue in st st until piece measures 1 ½" from cast on edge ending with a p row.
Armhole shaping:
Next row (rs): cast off 6 sts, k to end.
Next row (ws): cast off 6 sts, p to end.
There are now 32 (35, 40, 47, 52) sts remaining.
Next row (rs): k3, skp, k to last 5 sts, k2tog, k3.
Next row (ws): p.
Repeat last two rows until there are 8 (9, 10, 11, 12) sts remaining ending with a p row. Place sts on holder.

neckband
Place sts from holders onto a needle in the following order: back right, sleeve, front, sleeve, back left. There are now 60 (66, 72, 78, 84) sts.
Next row (rs): k10 (11, 12, 13, 14), k2tog, k2tog, k4 (5, 6, 7, 8), k2tog, k2tog, k16 (18, 20, 22, 24), k2tog, k2tog, k4 (5, 6, 7, 8), k2tog, k2tog, k10 (11, 12, 13, 14). There are now 52 (58, 64, 70, 76) sts remaining.
Next row: k.
Next row: k to last 3 sts, yo, k2tog, k1.
K two rows. Cast off.

finishing
Join raglan, arm and side seams. Sew buttons in place.

notes
The placket overlaps at the center. The overlap is created by sharing four stitches. Using the safety pin insures that you pick up and knit the stitches from the correct row.

bikini

materials	1 ball Brown Sheep Cotton Fleece in Nymph Pair of size US 6 14" knitting needles
gauge	20 sts and 28 rows = 4" square measured over st st using US 6 needles
size	2 (4, 6, 8, 10)
finished measurements	Width at bottom of triangle: 4 ½ (5, 5 ½, 6, 6 ½)" Height: 3 ½ (4, 4 ¼, 4 ½, 4 ¾)"

triangles	Cast on 22 (26, 28, 30, 32) sts.
	Beginning with a k row, continue in st st for two rows.
	Next two rows: k (this creates the fold over edge for lower casing).
	Next row (rs): k.
	Next row (ws): k2, p to last 2 sts, k2.
	Repeat these two rows one more time.
	Next row: k2, skp, k to last 4 sts, k2tog, k2.
	Next row: k2, p to last 2 sts, k2.
	Repeat these two rows until there are 6 sts remaining.
	
	Next row (rs):
	  For one triangle: k2, skp, k2.
	  For other triangle: k2, k2tog, k2.
	
	Both triangles continue:
	Next row (ws): k2, p1, k2.
	Next row: skp, k1, k2tog. There are now 3 sts remaining.
	Beginning with a p row, continue in st st until strap measures 14 (15, 16, 17, 18)" ending with a p row.
	Cast off.

finishing	Fold over lower edge and sew in place to form casing. Cut nine equal lengths of yarn 40 (42, 44, 46, 48)". Tie knot at end. Divide into three sections and braid tightly to end. Tie knot. Thread braided cord through casing.

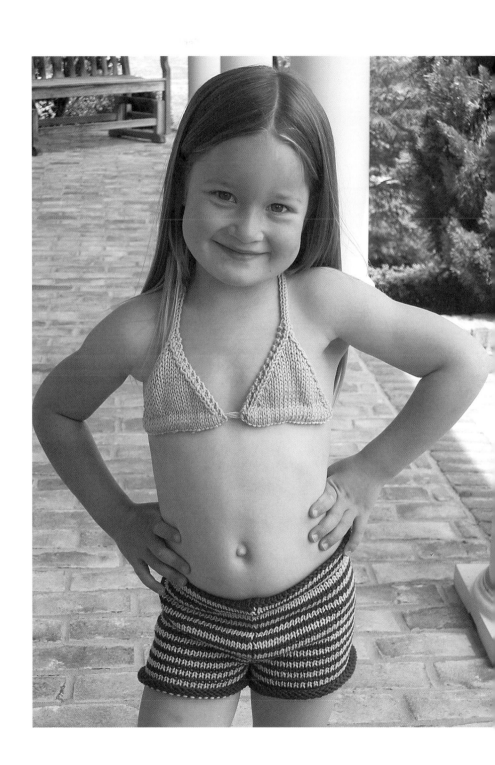

short shorts

The short shorts are knit from the bottom up. Wear them paired with the bikini top and be cool (pictured on page 8) or with a tee-shirt and look cool (pictured on page 23). The directions are given for the striped shorts.

materials	1 ball Brown Sheep Cotton Fleece in Truffle (A) 1 ball Brown Sheep Cotton Fleece in Nymph (B) (The above colors are for the striped shorts shown on page 8. If knitting shorts in one color, you will need 1 (1, 1, 2, 2) ball(s) of desired color. See notes below for colors used on pages 9 and 23). Pair of size US 6 14" knitting needles ⅝" elastic to fit waist
gauge	20 sts and 28 rows = 4" square measured over st st using US 6 needles
size	2 (4, 6, 8, 10)
finished measurements	Waist: 16 (19, 22, 25, 28)" Length: 6 ½ (7 ½, 8 ½, 9 ½, 10 ½)"
left & right sides alike	Cast on 52 (60, 68, 75, 84) sts with A. Beginning with a k row, continue in st st for four rows ending with a p row. Join in B and from this point on, throughout the pattern, alternate colors every two rows. Continue in st st for 4 (6, 6, 8, 8) rows ending with a p row. Crotch shaping: Cast off 3 sts at beginning of next two rows. There are now 46 (54, 62, 69, 78) sts remaining. Next row (rs): k1, skp, k to last 3 sts, k2tog, k1. Next row (ws): p. Repeat last two rows two more times ending with a p row. There are now 40 (48, 56, 63, 72) sts remaining. Continue in st st until piece measures 6 ½ (7 ½, 8 ½, 9 ½, 10 ½)" from cast on edge ending with a p row. Next three rows: k (this creates the fold over edge). Beginning with a p row, continue in st st for five rows ending with a p row. Cast off.
finishing	Join front, back and inside leg seams. Fold over upper edge and sew in place to form casing leaving a 2" opening. Thread elastic in casing being careful not to twist. Sew elastic to desired size and close casing.
notes	Short shorts photographed on page 9 are knit in Truffle and Coral Sunset. Short shorts on page 23 are knit in Caribbean Sea.

tankini

We can't think of anything the tankini would not look great with. Wear it with a pair of jeans or capris, long flared skirt, denim mini-skirt, white shorts - the list goes on.

materials	1 (1, 1, 2, 2) ball(s) Brown Sheep Cotton Fleece in Truffle (A) 1 ball Brown Sheep Cotton Fleece in Coral Sunset (B) Pair of size US 6 14" knitting needles
gauge	20 sts and 28 rows = 4" square measured over st st using US 6 needles
size	2 (4, 6, 8, 10)
finished measurements	Width at waist: 19 (21, 22 ½, 24, 25 ½)" Length from top of triangle to bottom edge: 10 (11 ½, 12 ¾, 14, 15 ½)"
back	Cast on 48 (52, 56, 60, 64) sts with A. Beginning with a k row, continue in st st until piece measures 6 (7, 8, 9, 10)" from cast on edge ending with a p row. Next row (rs): k1, [p2, k2], repeat to last 3 sts, p2, k1. Next row (ws): p1, [k2, p2], repeat to last 3 sts, k2, p1. Next row (rs): k1, [p2, k2], repeat to last 3 sts, p2, k1. Cast off in rib.
front	Cast on 48 (52, 56, 60, 64) sts with A. Beginning with a k row, continue in st st until piece measures 6 ½ (7 ½, 8 ½, 9 ½, 10 ½)" from cast on edge ending with a p row (front and back pieces will be the same length). Left triangle: Next row (rs): join in B, k22 (24, 26, 28, 30), place safety pin through next 4 sts on left hand needle, k these 4 sts (see notes below). Turn and work on these 26 (28, 30, 32, 34) sts only. Next row (ws): k2, p to last 2 sts, k2. Next row (rs): k2, skp, k to last 4 sts, k2tog, k2. Repeat these two rows until there are 6 sts remaining ending with a ws row. Next row (rs): k2, k2tog, k2. Next row (ws): k2, p1, k2. Next row (rs): k2tog, k1, k2tog. There are now 3 sts remaining. Next row (ws): p3. Next row (rs): k3. Repeat these two rows until strap measures 14 (15, 16, 17, 18)" ending with a p row. Cast off.

Right triangle:
Place 4 sts from safety pin on to left hand needle. There are now 26 (28, 30, 32, 34) sts on the left needle.
Next row (rs): join in B, k.
Next row (ws): k2, p to last 2 sts, k2.
Next row (rs): k2, skp, k to last 4 sts, k2tog, k2.
Repeat these two rows until there are 6 sts remaining ending with a ws row.
Next row (rs): k2, skp, k2.
Next row (ws): k2, p1, k2.
Next row (rs): k2tog, k1, k2tog. There are now 3 sts remaining.
Next row (ws): p3.
Next row (rs): k3.
Repeat these two rows until strap measures 14 (15, 16, 17, 18)" ending with a p row.
Cast off.

finishing

Join side seams.

notes

The triangles overlap at the center. The overlap is created by sharing four stitches. Using the safety pin insures that you pick up and knit the stitches from the correct row.

rumper

We are offering this piece in one size, not out of laziness on our part (PU-LEASE!!!) but because we feel it suits a smaller child's personality.

materials	2 balls Brown Sheep Cotton Fleece in Barn Red (A) 1 ball Brown Sheep Cotton Fleece in Cotton Ball (B) Pair of size US 6 14" knitting needles 1 yard ribbon
gauge	20 sts and 28 rows = 4" square measured over st st using US 6 needles
size	2
finished measurements	Chest: 23" Length: 19"
front & back	First leg: Cast on 38 sts with A. Row 1: [k2, p2], repeat to last 2 sts, k2. Row 2: [p2, k2], repeat to last 2 sts, p2. Repeat rows 1 and 2 one more time (bottom rib edge). Beginning with a k row, continue in st st until piece measures 2" from cast on edge ending with a p row. Crotch shaping: Next row (rs): cast off 3 sts, k to end. Next row (ws): p. Next row: k2, skp, k to end. Next row: p. Repeat last two rows two more times. There are now 32 sts remaining. Place sts on holder. Second leg: Cast on 38 sts with A. Row 1: [k2, p2], repeat to last 2 sts, k2. Row 2: [p2, k2], repeat to last 2 sts, p2. Repeat rows 1 and 2 one more time (bottom rib edge). Beginning with a k row, continue in st st until piece measures 2" from cast on edge ending with a k row. Crotch shaping: Next row (ws): cast off 3 sts, p to end. Next row: k to last 4 sts, k2tog k2. Next row: p. Repeat last two rows two more times. There are now 32 sts remaining.

Join left and right front legs:

Next row: k32, then k32 from holder. There are now 64 sts.

Beginning with a p row, continue in st st until piece measures 9" from cast on edge ending with a p row.

Next row (dec row): k2, skp, k to last 4 sts, k2tog, k2.

Beginning with a p row, continue in st st decreasing two sts (as in dec row) every 12th row until there are 58 sts remaining.

Continue in st st until piece measures 13 ¼" from cast on edge ending with a p row.

Next row: join in B, k.

Next row: p.

Next row (rs) eyelet row:

For front piece: k4, k2tog, yo, [k3, k2tog, yo] four times, k3, [k3, yo, k2tog] five times, k4.

For back piece: k1, [yo, k2tog, k3], repeat to last 2 sts, yo, k2tog.

Continue for front and back pieces:

Beginning with a p row, continue in st st until piece measures 14 ½" from cast on edge ending with a p row.

Armhole shaping:

Cast off 3 sts at beginning of next two rows. There are now 52 sts remaining.

Next row (dec row): k2, skp, k to last 4 sts, k2tog, k2.

Next row: p.

Repeat last two rows until there are 40 sts remaining ending with a p row.

Shoulder strap:

Next row: k2, skp, k to last 4 sts, k2tog, k2. There are now 38 sts remaining.

Next row: p11. Turn and work on these sts only.

Next row: k2tog, k to last 4 sts, k2tog, k2.

Next row: p.

Repeat last two rows two more times ending with a p row. There are now 5 sts remaining.

Continue in st st until piece measures 19" from cast on edge ending with a p row.

Cast off.

Other shoulder strap:

Place next 16 sts on holder (neck edge), p to end. There are 11 sts on the needle.

Next row: k2, skp, k to last 2 sts, k2tog.

Next row: p.

Repeat last two rows two more times ending with a p row. There are now 5 sts remaining.

Continue in st st until piece measures 19" from cast on edge ending with a p row.

Cast off.

armhole edging | Join side seams. With right side facing, pick up and k52 sts evenly along entire armhole.
Next row: k.
Cast off.
Repeat for other armhole.

neck edging | With right side facing, pick up and k13 down front slope, k16 from holder, pick up and k13 up front slope. There are now 42 sts.
Next row: k.
Cast off.
Repeat for back.

finishing | Join shoulder, crotch and inside leg seams.

knit down sweater

Like the knit down dress, this sweater begins at the neck and upper sleeve edge and is knit to the hem.

materials	1 (2, 2, 2, 3) ball(s) Brown Sheep Cotton Fleece in Cotton Ball (A) 2 (2, 3, 3, 3) balls Brown Sheep Cotton Fleece in Lapis (B) Pair of size US 6 14" knitting needles (see notes below)
gauge	20 sts and 28 rows = 4" square measured over st st using US 6 needles
size	2 (4, 6, 8, 10)
finished measurements	Armspan: 35 ½ (37 ½, 41 ½, 45 ½, 49 ½)" Chest: 23 (24 ½, 25, 26 ½, 28 ½)" Length: 14 ½ (16, 17 ½, 19, 20 ½)"
front & back alike	Cast on 177 (187, 207, 227, 247) sts with A. Row 1 (rs): [k7, p3], repeat to last 7 sts, k7. Row 2 (ws): [p7, k3], repeat to last 7 sts, p7. Repeat rows 1 and 2 until piece measures 3 (3 ½, 3 ½, 4, 4 ½)" from cast on edge ending with a ws row. At the beginning of next eight rows: cast off 15 (16, 18, 20, 22) sts in pattern, pattern to end. There are now 57 (59, 63, 67, 71) sts remaining. Next row (rs): join in B, beginning with a k row, continue in st st until piece measures 14 ½ (16, 17 ½, 19, 20 ½)" from cast on edge ending with a p row. Cast off.
finishing	Join shoulder seams leaving center 6 (6 ½, 7, 7 ½, 8)" opening for neck. Join sleeve and side seams.
notes	Casting on a large number of stitches on straight needles can be uncomfortable to work with. If you find this to be the case we suggest using circular needles for sizes 6, 8 and 10.

tank top

This is truly a top any girl can grow with. One of our children wore the tank top with the ruffle pants setting off a domino effect. Suddenly we were being asked to write instructions for our patterns. Thus began the start of *barefoot knits*!

materials	2 (2, 2, 3, 3) balls Brown Sheep Cotton Fleece in Lime Light (See notes below for colors used on pages 12 and 13) Pair of size US 6 14" knitting needles
gauge	20 sts and 28 rows = 4" square measured over st st using US 6 needles
size	2 (4, 6, 8, 10)
finished measurements	Chest: 23 (25 ½, 28, 30 ½, 33)" Length: 15 ½ (17 ½, 20 ½, 23, 26)"
front & back alike	Cast on 58 (64, 70, 76, 82) sts. K 4 (4, 6, 6, 6) rows. Beginning with a k row, continue in st st until piece measures 9 (10, 11, 12 ½, 14)" from cast on edge ending with a k row. Next row (ws): k3, p to last 3 sts, k3. Next row (rs): k. Next row: k6, p to last 6 sts, k6. Next row: k.

Armhole shaping:
Next row (ws): cast off 3 sts, k2, p to last 6 sts, k6.
Next row (rs): cast off 3 sts, k to end. There are now 52 (58, 64, 70, 76) sts remaining.
Next row: k3, p to last 3 sts, k3.
Next row: k3, skp, k to last 5 sts, k2tog, k3.
Repeat last two rows until there are 24 (26, 28, 32, 36) sts remaining ending with a k row.
Next row (ws): k.
Next row (rs): k3, skp, k to last 5 sts, k2tog, k3. There are now 22 (24, 26, 30, 34) sts remaining.
Next row: k.

Divide for straps:
Next row: k4, cast off 14 (16, 18, 22, 26) sts, k3. Turn and work on these 4 sts only (first strap).
Continue in garter st (k every row) until strap measures 1 ½ (2, 3, 4, 5)".
Cast off.

Join in yarn at neck edge (second strap).
Continue in garter st (k every row) until strap measures 1 ½ (2, 3, 4, 5)".
Cast off.

finishing   Join side and shoulder seams.

notes   Tank tops photographed on cover are knit in Cherry Moon and Lime Light. Tank tops photographed on pages 12 and 13 are knit in colors Lime Light, Wild Orange, Cherry Moon, Caribbean Sea.

ruffle pants

Wear these pants with the tank top year round. Try a white turtle neck in the winter, a short sleeve shirt in the spring and fall, and on its own for the summer.

materials	2 (2, 2, 3, 4) balls Brown Sheep Cotton Fleece in Caribbean Sea (A) 1 ball Brown Sheep Cotton Fleece in Lime Light (B) (See notes below for colors used on cover and page 12) Pair of sizeUS 6 14" knitting needles (see notes below) ⅝" elastic to fit waist
gauge	20 sts and 28 rows = 4" square measured over st st using US 6 needles
size	2 (4, 6, 8, 10)
finished measurements	Waist: 16 (19, 22, 25, 28)" Inseam: 13 (18, 21, 24, 27)"
left & right alike	Cast on 156 (180, 204, 225, 252) sts with A. P eight rows. Next row: join in B, k3tog to end. There are now 52 (60, 68, 75, 84) sts remaining. Next row: p. Row 1: join in A, k. Row 2: p. Row 3: k. Row 4: p. Row 5: k. Row 6: p. Row 7: k. Row 8: p. Row 9: join in B, k. Row 10: p. Keeping stripe pattern correct, continue in st st until piece measures 13 (18, 21, 24, 26)" from cast on edge ending with a p row. Crotch shaping: Cast off 3 sts at beginning of next two rows. There are now 46 (54, 62, 69, 78) sts remaining. Next row: k1, skp, k to last 3 sts, k2tog, k1. Next row: p. Repeat last two rows two more times ending with a p row. There are now 40 (48, 56, 63, 72) sts remaining. Continue in st st until piece measures 18 ½ (24, 29, 33, 36)" from cast on edge ending with a p row. Next three rows: k (this creates the fold over edge).

Beginning with a p row, continue in st st for five rows ending with a p row.
Cast off.

finishing

Join front, back and inside leg seams. Fold over upper edge and sew in place to form casing leaving a 2" opening. Thread elastic in casing being careful not to twist. Sew elastic to desired size and close casing.

notes

Pants photographed on cover are knit in Caribbean Sea and Lime Light. Pants photographed on page 12 and 13 are knit in Caribbean Sea and Lime Light; Cherry Moon and Wild Orange.

Casting on a large number of stitches on straight needles can be uncomfortable to work with. If you find this to be the case, we suggest using circular needles for sizes 6, 8 and 10.

ruffle skirt

materials	1 (2, 2, 2, 3) ball(s) Brown Sheep Cotton Fleece in Wild Orange (A) 1 ball Brown Sheep Cotton Fleece in Cherry Moon (B) (see notes below) Pair of size US 6 14" knitting needles (see notes below) ⅝" elastic to fit around waist
gauge	20 sts and 28 rows = 4" square measured over st st using US 6 needles
size	2 (4, 6, 8, 10)
finished measurements	Waist: 16 (19, 22, 25, 28)" Length: 9 (11, 13, 15, 17)"
front & back alike	Cast on 138 (162, 192, 213, 240) sts with A. P eight rows. Next row: join in B, k3tog to end. There are now 46 (54, 64, 71, 80) sts remaining. Next row: p. Row 1: join in A, k. Row 2: p. Row 3: k. Row 4: p. Row 5: k. Row 6: p. Row 7: k. Row 8: p. Row 9: join in B, k. Row 10: p. Next row (dec row): join in A, k2, skp, k to last 4 sts, k2tog, k2. Keeping stripe pattern correct, continue in st st decreasing two sts (as in dec row) every 14th (16th, 16th, 20th, 22nd) row until there are 40 (48, 56, 63, 72) sts remaining. Continue in st st until piece measures 9 (11, 13, 15, 17)" from cast on edge ending with a p row. Next three rows: k (this creates the fold over edge). Beginning with a p row, continue in st st for five rows ending with a p row. Cast off.
finishing	Join side seams. Fold over upper edge and sew in place to form casing leaving a 2" opening. Thread elastic in casing being careful not to twist. Sew elastic to desired size and close casing.
notes	Skirt photographed on cover is knit in Wild Orange and Cherry Moon. Skirts photographed on page 12 and 13 are knit in Wild Orange and Cherry Moon; Lime Light and Caribbean Sea. Casting on a large number of stitches on straight needles can be uncomfortable to work with. If you find this to be the case, we suggest using circular needles for sizes 8 and 10.

baby blanket

Can you think of one mother that wouldn't love to receive a blanket like this for her baby shower? If you are knitting for a little girl, we suggest Tea Rose, Pink-a-Boo and Cotton Ball. If you would like to knit gender neutral, try Holly Green, Lime Light and Putty.

materials	2 balls Brown Sheep Cotton Fleece in Wolverine Blue (A) 2 balls Brown Sheep Cotton Fleece in Nymph (B) 2 balls Brown Sheep Cotton Fleece in Putty (C) Pair of size US 6 14" knitting needles
gauge	20 sts and 28 rows = 4" square measured over st st using US 6 needles
finished measurements	36 x 41"
blanket	Cast on 180 sts with A. K six rows (garter edge). Row 1 (rs): k. Row 2 (ws): k5, p to last 5 sts, k5. Repeat rows 1 and 2, 20 more times ending with a ws row. Join in B and repeat rows 1 and 2 above 24 times. Join in C and repeat rows 1 and 2 above 24 times. Join in A and repeat rows 1 and 2 above 24 times. Join in B and repeat rows 1 and 2 above 24 times. Join in C and repeat rows 1 and 2 above 21 times. K six rows (garter edge). Cast off.

lace-up cardigan

What makes this cardigan so unique are the bell shaped sleeves and the lace-up closure. For a casual look, wear the cardigan with jeans or for a formal occasion, pair it with a velvet skirt. We'll leave the choice to go barefoot to a formal occasion entirely up to you!

materials	3 (3, 4, 5, 5) balls Brown Sheep Cotton Fleece in New Age Teal Pair of size US 6 14" knitting needles 1 yard ribbon
gauge	20 sts and 28 rows = 4" square measured over st st using US 6 needles
size	2 (4, 6, 8, 10)
finished measurements	Chest: 24 (26 ½, 28, 30 ½, 32)" Length: 15 ½ (17, 18, 20, 22)"
back	Cast on 70 (76, 82, 90, 98) sts. K four rows. Beginning with a k row, continue in st st for ten rows ending with a p row. Next row (dec row): k2, skp, k to last 4 sts, k2tog, k2. Beginning with a p row, continue in st st decreasing 2 sts (as in dec row) every 14th (16th, 14th, 16th, 16th) row until there are 60 (66, 70, 78, 84) sts remaining ending with a p row. Continue in st st until piece measures 11 (12, 13, 15, 17)" from cast on edge ending with a p row. Armhole shaping: Cast off 5 (5, 5, 6, 6) sts at beginning of next two rows. There are now 50 (56, 60, 66, 72) sts remaining. Next row (rs): k3, skp, k to last 5 sts, k2tog, k3. Next row (ws): p. Repeat last two rows until there are 22 (24, 26, 30, 34) sts remaining ending with a p row. Cast off.
right front	Cast on 35 (38, 41, 45, 49) sts. K five rows. Next row (ws): p to last 3 sts, k3 (this creates the vertical garter edge). Next row (rs): k. Repeat last two rows three more times ending with a rs row. Next row (ws): p to last 3 sts, k3. Next row (dec row): k to last 4 sts, k2tog, k2. While maintaining garter edge throughout, continue in st st decreasing 1 st (as in dec row) every 14th (16th, 14th, 16th, 16th) row until there are 30 (33, 35, 39, 42) sts remaining ending with a p row.

Continue in st st until piece measures 11 (12, 13, 15, 17)" from cast on edge ending with a p row.

Armhole shaping:
Next row (rs): k.
Next row (ws): cast off 5 (5, 5, 6, 6) sts, p to last 3 sts, k3. There are now 25 (28, 30, 33, 36) sts remaining.
Next row: k to last 5 sts, k2tog, k3.
Next row: p to last 3 sts, k3.
Next row: k1, k2tog, yo, k to last 5 sts, k2tog, k3 (this creates hole).
Next row: p to last 3 sts, k3.
Next row: k to last 5 sts, k2tog, k3.
Next row: p to last 3 sts, k3.
Next row: k1, k2tog, yo, k to last 5 sts, k2tog, k3 (this creates second hole).
Next row: p to last 3 sts, k3.
Next row: k to last 5 sts, k2tog, k3.
Next row: p to last 3 sts, k3.
Next row: k1, k2tog, yo, k to last 5 sts, k2tog, k3 (this creates third hole).
Next row: p to last 3 sts, k3.
Next row: k to last 5 sts, k2tog, k3.
Next row: p to last 3 sts, k3.
Next row: k3, skp, k to last 5 sts, k2tog, k3.
Repeat last two rows until there are 10 (11, 11, 10, 9) sts remaining.
Next row: p to last 3 sts, k3.
Next row: k to last 5 sts, k2tog, k3.
Repeat last two rows until there are 7 sts remaining.
Next row: p to last 3 sts, k3.
Next row: k3, cast off to end.
Place remaining 3 sts on holder.

left front

Cast on 35 (38, 41, 45, 49) sts.
K five rows.
Next row (ws): k3, p to end (this creates the vertical garter edge).
Next row (rs): k.
Repeat last two rows three more times ending with a rs row.
Next row (ws): k3, p to end.
Next row (dec row): k2, skp, k to end.
While maintaining garter edge throughout, continue in st st decreasing 2 sts (as in dec row) every 14th (16th, 14th, 16th, 16th) row until there are 30 (33, 35, 39, 42) sts remaining ending with a p row.
Continue in st st until piece measures 11 (12, 13, 15, 17)" from cast on edge ending with a p row.

Armhole shaping:
Next row (rs): cast off 5 (5, 5, 6, 6) sts, k to end. There are now 25 (28, 30, 33, 36) sts remaining.
Next row (ws): k3, p to end.
Next row: k3, skp, k to end.
Next row: k3, p to end.

77

Next row: k3, skp, k to last 3 sts, yo, k2tog, k1 (this creates hole).
Next row: k3, p to end.
Next row: k3, skp, k to end.
Next row: k3, p to end.
Next row: k3, skp, k to last 3 sts, yo, k2tog, k1 (this creates second hole).
Next row: k3, p to end.
Next row: k3, skp, k to end.
Next row: k3, p to end.
Next row: k3, skp, k to last 3 sts, yo, k2tog, k1 (this creates third hole).
Next row: k3, p to end.
Next row: k3, skp, k to end.
Next row: k3, p to end.
Next row: k3, skp, k to last 5 sts, k2tog, k3.
Repeat last two rows until there are 10 (11, 11, 10, 9) sts remaining.
Next row: k3, p to end.
Next row: k3, skp, k to end.
Repeat last two rows until there are 7 sts remaining.
Next row: k3, p to end.
Next row: cast off 4 sts, k2.
Place remaining 3 sts on holder.

sleeves
make 2 alike

Cast on 52 (56, 61, 67, 69) sts.
K four rows.
Beginning with a k row, continue in st st for 4 (6, 4, 6, 8) rows ending with a p row.
Next row (dec row): k2, skp, k to last 4 sts, k2tog, k2.
Beginning with a p row, continue in st st decreasing 2 sts (as in dec row) every 10th (12th, 10th, 12th, 14th) row until there are 44 (48, 51, 57, 59) sts remaining ending with a p row.
Continue in st st for 10 (8, 6, 8, 6) rows ending with a p row.
Next row (inc row): k2, m1rs, k to last 2 sts, m1ls, k2.
Beginning with a p row, continue in st st increasing 2 sts (as in inc row) every 10th (12th, 10th, 12th, 14th) row until there are 50 (54, 59, 65, 67) sts.
Continue in st st until piece measures 11 (12, 13, 15, 17)" from cast on edge ending with a p row.

Armhole shaping:
Cast off 5 (5, 5, 6, 6) sts at beginning of next two rows. There are now 40 (44, 49, 53, 55) sts.
Next row (rs): k3, skp, k to last 5 sts, k2tog, k3.
Next row (ws): p.
Repeat last two rows until there are 12 (12, 15, 17, 17) sts remaining ending with a p row.
Cast off.

finishing

Join raglan, side and arm seams. Join yarn and k3 sts from holder.
Continue in garter st until length of neck band matches center back edge.
Cast off. Repeat for other side. Stitch neckband in place meeting other side neckband at back center.

long skirt

This skirt is knit in two pieces beginning at the waist and continuing to the hem. The skirt can be worn in two ways: with the seams on the side giving an A-line shape, or, as pictured, with the seams in the front and back giving the skirt a V-shaped waist and hemline (worn this way, the length increases).

materials	2 (3, 3, 4, 4) balls Brown Sheep Cotton Fleece in Cotton Ball (See notes below for colors used on pages 41 and 42) Pair of size US 6 14" knitting needles
gauge	20 sts and 28 rows = 4" square measured over st st using US 6 needles
size	2 (4, 6, 8, 10)
finished measurements	Waist: 18 (20, 22, 24, 26)" Length: 16 (18, 20, 22, 24)" when skirt seams are on the side

front & back	Cast on 45 (50, 55, 60, 65) sts.
	K four rows.
	
	Next row (eyelet row):
	    For front piece: k4, [yo, k2tog, k3], repeat to last st, k1.
	    For back piece: k4, [k2tog, yo, k3], repeat to last st, k1.
	
	Both pieces continue:
	Row 1: k2, m1rs, k to last 2 sts, m1ls, k2.
	Row 2: p.
	Row 3: k.
	Row 4: p.
	Repeat rows 1 to 4 until piece measures 15 ½ (17 ½, 19 ½, 21 ½, 23 ½)" from cast on edge (measuring at center of piece).
	Next row: k2, m1rs, k to last 2 sts, m1ls, k2.
	Next four rows: k.
	Cast off.

finishing	Join seams. Cut nine equal lengths of yarn 38 (40, 42, 44, 46)". Tie knot at end. Divide into three sections and braid tightly to end. Tie knot. Thread braided cord through eyelet row.
notes	Striped skirt photographed on page 41 is knit in colors Perry's Primrose and Pink-a-Boo (alternating colors every eight rows). Skirt photographed on page 42 is knit in Cotton Ball and tie-dyed in lime (refer to page 51 for tie-dye instructions).

rugby sweater

This sweater would look great in your child's school colors. For a more girly color combination, knit it in Silver Plum and Victorian Pink.

materials	2 (2, 2, 3, 3) balls Brown Sheep Cotton Fleece in Wolverine Blue (A)
	2 (2, 2, 3, 3) balls Brown Sheep Cotton Fleece in Gold Dust (B)
	Pair of size US 6 14" knitting needles
	2 (2, 2, 3, 3) buttons
gauge	20 sts and 28 rows = 4" square measured over st st using US 6 needles
size	2 (4, 6, 8, 10)
finished measurements	Chest: 26 (28 ½, 30 ½, 33, 35 ½)"
	Length: 14 (16, 19, 22, 25)"
back	Cast on 65 (71, 77, 83, 89) with A.

back

Cast on 65 (71, 77, 83, 89) with A.
Row 1: p4 (2, 0, 3, 1), [k7, p3], repeat to last 1 (9, 7, 10, 8) st(s), p1 (0, 0, 0, 0), k0 (7, 7, 7, 7), p0 (2, 0, 3, 1).
Row 2: k1 (2, 0, 3, 1), p0 (7, 7, 7, 7), [k3, p7], repeat to last 4 (2, 0, 3, 1) st(s), k4 (2, 0, 3, 1).
Repeat rows 1 and 2, four more times.
Join in B, beginning with a k row, continue in st st for ten rows.
Join in A, beginning with a k row, continue in st st for ten rows.
Continue in st st, alternating colors every ten rows until piece measures 9 (11, 13, 15, 17)" from cast on edge ending with a p row.

Armhole shaping:
Cast off 4 (4, 4, 5, 5) sts at beginning of next two rows. There are now 57 (63, 69, 73, 79) sts remaining.
Continue in st st until piece measures 14 (16, 19, 22, 25)" from cast on edge ending with a p row.
Cast off 19 (21, 23, 25, 27) sts, k18 (20, 22, 22, 24), cast off to end.
Place center 19 (21, 23, 23, 25) sts on holder.

front

Cast on 65 (71, 77, 83, 89), with A.
Row 1: p4 (2, 0, 3, 1), [k7, p3], repeat to last 1 (9, 7, 10, 8) st(s), p1 (0, 0, 0, 0), k0 (7, 7, 7, 7), p0 (2, 0, 3, 1).
Row 2: k1 (2, 0, 3, 1), p0 (7, 7, 7, 7), [k3, p7], repeat to last 4 (2, 0, 3, 1) st(s), k4 (2, 0, 3, 1).
Repeat rows 1 and 2, four more times.
Join in B, beginning with a k row, continue in st st for ten rows.
Join in A, beginning with a k row, continue in st st for ten rows.
Continue in st st, alternating colors every ten rows until piece measures 9 (11, 13, 15, 17)" from cast on edge ending with a p row.

Armhole shaping:
Cast off 4 (4, 4, 5, 5) sts at beginning of next two rows. There are now 57 (63, 69, 73, 79) sts remaining.
Continue in st st until piece measures 9 ½ (12, 14, 16, 18)" from cast on edge ending with a p row.

Divide for placket (left side):
Row 1 (rs): k26 (29, 32, 34, 37), place safety pin through next 5 sts on left hand needle, k these 5 sts (see notes below). Turn and work on these 31 (34, 37, 39, 42) sts only.
Row 2 (ws): k5, p to end.
Row 3: k.
Row 4: k5, p to end.
Row 5: k.
Row 6: k5, p to end.
Row 7: k.
Row 8 (buttonhole): k1, k2tog, yo, k2, p to end.
Row 9: k.
Row 10: k5, p to end.
Row 11: k.
Repeat rows 2 to 11, 1 (1, 1, 2, 2) more time(s).
Next row: k5, p to end.
Next row: k.

Shape neck:
Next row (ws): cast off 5 sts, p to end.
Next row: k.
Next row: cast off 3 (3, 3, 3, 4) sts, p to end.
Next row: k.
Next row: cast off 3 sts, p to end.
Next row: k.
Next row: cast off 1 (2, 3, 3, 3) st(s), p to end. There are now 19 (21, 23, 25, 27) sts remaining.
Next row: k.
Continue in st st until piece measures 14 (16, 19, 22, 25)" from cast on edge ending with a p row.
Cast off.

Right side placket:
Place 5 sts from safety pin on to left hand needle. There are now 31 (34, 37, 39, 42) sts on the left needle.
Row 1 (rs): join in yarn, k.
Row 2 (ws): p to last 5 sts, k5.
Repeat rows 1 and 2, 10 (10, 10, 15, 15) more times.
Next row (rs): cast off 5 sts, k to end.
Next row: p.
Next row: cast off 3 (3, 3, 3, 4) sts, k to end.
Next row: p.
Next row: cast off 3 sts, k to end.
Next row: p.

Next row: cast off 1 (2, 3, 3, 3) st(s), k to end. There are now 19 (21, 23, 25, 27) sts remaining.
Next row: p.
Continue in st st until piece measures 14 (16, 19, 22, 25)" from cast on edge ending with a k row.
Cast off.

sleeves
make 2 alike

Cast on 38 (42, 42, 42, 44) sts with A.
Row 1: [k7, p3], repeat to last 8 (2, 2, 2, 4) sts, k7 (2, 2, 2, 4), p1 (0, 0, 0, 0).
Row 2: k1 (0, 0, 0, 0), p7 (2, 2, 2, 4), [k3, p7], repeat to end.
Repeat rows 1 and 2, four more times.
Join in B.
Next row (inc row): k2, m1ls, k to last 2 sts, m1rs, k2.
Beginning with a p row, continue in st st increasing two sts (as in inc row) every 12th (10th, 8th, 8th, 8th) row (alternating colors every ten rows) until there are 50 (60, 70, 80, 90) sts ending with a p row.
Continue in st st until piece measures 13 (15, 18, 21, 24)" from cast on edge ending with a p row.
Cast off.

collar

Join shoulder seams. With right side facing, starting after placket, pick up and k10 (13, 17, 19, 19) sts to shoulder, k13 (17, 23, 25, 25) sts from holder, pick up and k10 (13, 17, 19, 19) sts down front ending before placket.
K 20 (20, 20, 30, 30) rows.
Cast off.

finishing

Join sleeves at shoulders. Join side and arm seams. Sew buttons in place.

notes

The placket overlaps at the center. The overlap is created by sharing five stitches. Using the safety pin insures that you pick up and knit the stitches from the correct row.

three tier skirt

This skirt is reminiscent of western skirts. The graduation of colors from darker to lighter makes the skirt a treasure. Another fun color combination is Perry's Primrose, Tea Rose and Pink-A-Boo. The tree tier skirt is knit beginning at the lower picot edge.

materials	2 (2, 2, 2, 3) balls Brown Sheep Cotton Fleece in Harvest (A) 1 (2, 2, 2, 3) ball(s) Brown Sheep Cotton Fleece in Gold Dust (B) 1 (1, 1, 1, 2) ball(s) Brown Sheep Cotton Fleece in Buttercream (C) Pair of size US 6 14" knitting needles ⅝" elastic to fit waist
gauge	20 sts and 28 rows = 4" square measured over st st using US 6 needles
size	2 (4, 6, 8, 10)
finished measurements	Waist: 16 (19, 22 ½, 25 ½, 29)" Length: 13 (15 ½, 18, 21, 23 ½)"
front & back alike	Cast on 90 (108, 126, 144, 162) sts with A. Next row: k. Next row: p. Next row (picot row): k1, [k2tog, yo], repeat to last st, k1. Beginning with a p row, continue in st st for five rows ending with a p row. Next two rows: k. Beginning with a k row, continue in st st for 30 (36, 42, 48, 54) rows ending with a p row. Next row (rs): join in B, k1, [k3tog, k3], repeat to last 5 sts, k3tog, k2. There are now 60 (72, 84, 96, 108) sts remaining. Beginning with a p row, continue in st st for 31 (37, 43, 49, 55) rows ending with a p row. Next row (rs): join in C, k1, [k3tog, k3], repeat to last 5 sts, k3tog, k2. There are now 40 (48, 56, 64, 72) sts remaining. Beginning with a p row, continue in st st for 29 (35, 41, 47, 53) rows ending with a p row. Next three rows: k (this creates the fold over edge). Beginning with a p row, continue in st st for five rows ending with a p row. Cast off.
finishing	Join side seams. Fold over lower picot edge onto wrong side and sew in place. Fold over upper edge and sew in place to form casing leaving a 2" opening. Thread elastic in casing being careful not to twist. Sew elastic to desired size and close casing.

spiral skirt

This whimsical skirt is knit beginning at the waist and continuing to the hem. The spiral on the bottom edge is created by increasing stitches with yarn overs.

materials	2 (2, 2, 3, 3) balls Brown Sheep Cotton Fleece in My Blue Heaven Pair of size US 6 14" knitting needles (see notes below) ⅝" elastic to fit waist
gauge	20 sts and 28 rows = 4" square measured over st st using US 6 needles
size	2 (4, 6, 8, 10)
finished measurements	Waist: 17 (20, 22 ½, 25 ½, 27)" Length: 12 (14, 16, 18, 20)"
front & back alike	Cast on 42 (50, 56, 64, 68) sts. Beginning with a k row, continue in st st for four rows ending with a p row. Next three rows: k (this creates the fold over edge). Beginning with a p row, continue in st st for 3 (5, 7, 9, 11) rows ending with a p row. Next row (inc row): k2, m1rs, k to last 2 sts, m1ls, k2. Beginning with a p row, continue in st st increasing two sts (as in inc row) every 4th (6th, 8th, 10th, 12th) rows until there are 48 (56, 64, 72, 76) sts. Next row: p. Beginning with a k row, continue in st st until piece measures 9 ½ (11 ½, 13 ½, 15 ½, 17 ½)" from fold over edge ending with a p row. Sprial shaping: Next row (rs): [k4, yo], repeat to last 4 sts, k4. Next row: p. Next row (rs): [k5, yo], repeat to last 4 sts, k4. Next row: p. Next row (rs): [k6, yo], repeat to last 4 sts, k4. Next row: p. Next row (rs): [k7, yo], repeat to last 4 sts, k4. Next row: p. Next row (rs): [k8, yo], repeat to last 4 sts, k4. Next row: p. Next row (rs): [k9, yo], repeat to last 4 sts, k4. Next row: p. Next row (rs): [k10, yo], repeat to last 4 sts, k4. Next row: p. Next row (rs): [k11, yo], repeat to last 4 sts, k4. Next row: p. Next row (rs): [k12, yo], repeat to last 4 sts, k4. There are now 147 (173, 199, 225, 238) sts.

Next row: k.
Cast off knitwise.

finishing

Join side seams. Fold over upper edge and sew in place to form casing leaving a 2" opening. Thread elastic in casing being careful not to twist. Sew elastic to desired size and close casing.

notes

As you begin working the spiral edge the number of sts increases significantly. A large number of stitches on straight needles can be uncomfortable to work with. If you find this to be the case we suggest switching to circular needles for sizes 6, 8 and 10.

drawstring backpack

materials	1 ball Brown Sheep Cotton Fleece in Nymph (A) 1 ball Brown Sheep Cotton Fleece in Mariner Blue (B) Pair of size US 6 14" knitting needles
gauge	20 sts and 28 rows = 4" square measured over st st using US 6 needles
finished measurements	9 ½ x 10 ½"
front & back alike	Cast on 48 sts with A. Beginning with a k row, continue in st st for six rows ending with a p row. Next three rows: k (this creates the fold over edge at the top of bag). Beginning with a p row, continue in st st for three rows ending with a p row. Next row (hole row): k3, yo, k2tog, k to last 5 sts, k2tog, yo, k3. Beginning with a p row, continue in st st for three rows ending with a p row. Row 1: join in B, k. Row 2: p. Row 3: k. Row 4: p. Row 5: k. Row 6: p. Row 7: k. Row 8: p. Row 9: join in A, k. Row 10: k. Repeat rows 1 to 10 five more times. Next row: join in B, k. Beginning with a p row, continue in st st for seven rows ending with a p row. Cast off.
finishing	Join side and bottom seams. Fold over upper edge and sew in place to form casing. Make two I-cords 50" long (refer to page 51 for I-cord instructions). Beginning on one side, thread I cord through entire casing exiting on same side. Repeat for other side. Attach cords to bottom corners of backpack.

tic tac toe pouch

This pouch will easily entertain all children. The two year old child will love playing with the pieces, while the older child will enjoy playing the game. Bonus: no need to keep drawing the lines.

materials	1 ball Brown Sheep Cotton Fleece in Wild Orange (A) 1 ball Brown Sheep Cotton Fleece in Raging Purple (B) Pair of size US 6 14" knitting needles Five "X" pieces and five "O" pieces 9" zipper
gauge	20 sts and 28 rows = 4" square measured over st st using US 6 needles
finished measurements	10 x 8 ½"
front	Cast on 50 sts with A. Beginning with a k row, continue in st st for nine rows ending with a k row. Row 1: p18 (A), p2 (B), p10 (A), p2 (B), p18 (A). Row 2: k18 (A), k2 (B), k10 (A), k2 (B), k18 (A). Repeat these two rows six times more. Next row: p8 (A), p34 (B), p3 (A). Next row: k8 (A), k34 (B), k3 (A). Repeat rows 1 and 2 above, seven times. Next row: p8 (A), p34 (B), p3 (A). Next row: k8 (A), k34 (B), k3 (A). Repeat rows 1 and 2 above, seven times. Beginning with a p row, continue in st st for nine rows ending with a p row. There are a total of 64 rows worked. Cast off.
back	Cast on 50 sts with A. Beginning with a k row, continue in st st alternating colors A and B every two rows working a total of 64 rows ending with p row. Cast off.
finishing	Join side and bottom seams. Attach zipper to top edge.

halter top

The halter top is a fun, quick and simple piece to knit. The top is knit in one piece beginning at the bottom edge including the straps, and ending at the upper edge. It is pictured on the back cover tie-dyed in navy and hot pink.

materials	1 ball Brown Sheep Cotton Fleece in Wisteria (See notes below for colors used on pages 24 and 25) Pair of size US 6 14" knitting needles
gauge	20 sts and 28 rows = 4" square measured over st st using US 6 needles
size	Small: 2/4 (Medium: 6/8, Large: 10/12)
finished measurements	Bottom edge width without straps: 13 (17 ½, 21 ½)" Height: 8 (10 ½, 12 ½)"
halter	Cast on 136 (167, 198) sts. K six rows. Next two rows: cast off 35 (40, 45) sts, k to end. There are now 66 (87, 108) sts remaining (this forms the straps). Next row (rs): k2, skp, k to last 4 sts, k2tog, k2. Next row (ws): p. Repeat these two rows until there are 18 (23, 28) sts remaining ending with a p row. Next three rows: k (this creates the fold over edge for casing). Beginning with a p row, continue in st st for three rows ending with a p row. Cast off.
finishing	Fold over upper edge and sew in place to form casing. Cut nine equal lengths of yarn 29 (31, 33)". Tie knot at end. Divide into three sections and braid to end. Tie knot. Thread braided cord through casing edge.
notes	Halter tops photographed on pages 24 and 25 are knit in Cotton Ball and tie-dyed in hot pink and navy blue (refer to page 51 for tie-dye instructions).

halter dress

materials	1 (1, 2, 2, 2) ball(s) Brown Sheep Cotton Fleece in Wisteria (A) 1 (1, 1, 2, 2) ball(s) Brown Sheep Cotton Fleece in Tea Rose (B) Pair of size US 6 14" knitting needles 1 ⅝" brass 'D' ring
gauge	20 sts and 28 rows = 4" square measured over st st using US 6 needles
size	2 (4, 6, 8, 10)
finished measurements	Chest: 18 ½ (20, 21 ½, 23, 25)" Back length: 16 (17 ½, 19, 21, 23)"
back	Cast on 58 (64, 70, 76, 82) sts with A. Beginning with a k row, continue in st st for 16 rows ending with a p row. Next row (dec row): k2, skp, k to last 2 sts, k2tog, k2. Beginning with a p row, continue in st st decreasing two sts (as in dec row) every 16th (16th, 14th, 14th, 14th) row until piece measures 9 (10, 11, 12, 13)" from cast on edge ending with a p row. Next row (rs): join in B, k. Continue in st st and decreasing as before until there are 46 (50, 54, 58, 62) sts remaining. Continue in st st until piece measures 15 ¼ (16 ¾, 18 ¼, 20 ¼, 22 ¼)" from cast on edge ending with a p row. Next row (rs): [k2, p2], repeat to last 2 sts, k2. Next row (ws): [p2, k2], repeat to last 2 sts, p2. Repeat last two rows one more time. Next row (rs): cast off 8 (8, 12, 12, 12) sts in rib, k1, p2, k2, cast off center 18 (22, 18, 22, 26) sts in rib, k1, p2, k2, cast off remaining sts in rib (you will have 12 sts on the needle, 6 for each strap). Place sts on holder.
front	Cast on 58 (64, 70, 76, 82) sts with A. Beginning with a k row, continue in st st for 16 rows ending with a p row. Next row (dec row): k2, skp, k to last 2 sts, k2tog, k2. Beginning with a p row, continue in st st decreasing two sts (as in dec row) every 16th (16th, 14th, 14th, 14th) row. Continue in st st until piece measures 9 (10, 11, 12, 13)" from cast on edge ending with a p row. Next row (rs): join in B, k. Continue in st st and decreasing as before until there are 46 (50, 54, 58, 62) sts remaining. Continue in st st until piece measures 16 (17 ½, 19, 21, 23)" from cast on edge ending with a p row (you will have worked the same number of rows as for the back up to the cast off edge). Next row: k. Next row: p.

Next row: k2, skp, k2, skp, k to last 8 sts, k2tog, k2, k2tog, k2.
Next row: p.
Repeat last two rows until there are 14 sts remaining ending with a p row.
Next row: k2, skp, k1, skp, k2tog, k1, k2tog, k2 . There are now 10 sts remaining.
Next two rows: k (this creates the fold over edge).
Next row: p.
Cast off.

straps

Working each strap from back piece separately, with right side facing, join yarn, k2, p2, k2 from holder.
Next row (ws): p2, k2, p2.
Next row (rs): k2, p2, k2.
Repeat these two rows until strap measures 7 (7 ½, 8, 8 ½, 9)" ending with a ws row.
Cast off in rib.
Join yarn to other side and work to match first strap.

finishing

Join side seams. Fold front top over 'D' ring at casing edge and sew in place. Fold straps over 'D' ring and sew each in place.

lace-up poncho

This poncho is knit in two triangular pieces beginning at the lower center point. The ribbon laced along the arm gives this poncho an edge over others.

materials	2 (3, 4) balls Brown Sheep Cotton Fleece in Pink-a-Boo Pair of size US 6 14" knitting needles 2 lengths of ribbon each 48"
gauge	20 sts and 28 rows = 4" square measured over st st using US 6 needles
size	2 (4, 6)
finished measurements	Armspan: 26 ½ (30, 33 ½)" Length: 18 ½ (21, 23 ½)"
poncho make 2 alike	Cast on 3 sts. K two rows. Next row (rs): k1, m1rs, k1, m1ls, k1 (5 sts). Next row (ws): k. Next row: k1, m1rs, k3, m1ls, k1 (7 sts). Next row: k. Next row: k1, m1rs, k5, m1ls, k1 (9 sts). Next row (ws): k3, p to last 3 sts, k3. Next row (rs): k4, m1rs, k to last 4 sts, m1ls, k4. Repeat last two rows until there are 129 (145, 163) sts ending with a p row. Next row: k4, m1rs, [yo, k2tog, k1] 15 (17, 19) times, k31 (35, 41), [k1, k2tog, yo] 15 (17, 19) times, m1ls, k4 (this row creates the holes for the lace up on both shoulder sides). Next row: k. Next row: k4, m1rs, k to last 4 sts, m1ls, k4. Next row: k. Cast off.
finishing	Join left and right shoulder seams. Poncho should be blocked into a triangular shape before lacing ribbon. Beginning at the neck edge, lace ribbon to form 'x's. Repeat for other side.

tank dress

This casual and care-free dress can be worn for many seasons, beginning as a longer dress and ending as a knee length dress years later. Don't be intimidated by the instructions - simply map out what needs to be done (see notes below). Once you get going, this is a simple dress to make.

materials	3 (3, 4, 4, 5) balls Brown Sheep Cotton Fleece in Terracotta Canyon Pair of size US 6 14" knitting needles
gauge	20 sts and 28 rows = 4" square measured over st st using US 6 needles
size	2 (4, 6, 8, 10)
finished measurements	Chest: 24 ½ (26, 27 ½, 29, 31)" Length: 24 ½ (29 ½, 34 ½, 37, 41)"

front & back alike

Cast on 85 (87, 89, 93, 97) sts.
Row 1: [k1, p1], repeat to last st, k1.
Repeat row 1 three more times (this creates seed st edge).
Beginning with a k row, continue in st st for four rows ending with a p row.
Next row (dot row): [k7, p1], repeat to last 5 (7, 1, 5, 1) st(s), k5 (7, 1, 5, 1).
Beginning with a p row, continue in st st for five rows ending with a p row.
Next and every following 10th (14th, 18th, 20th, 22nd) row (dec row): k2, skp, k to last 4 sts, k2tog, k2.
Beginning with a p row, continue in st st for three rows ending with a p row.
Next row (staggered dot row): k2, [p1, k7], repeat to last 1 (3, 5, 1, 5) st(s), k1 (3, 5, 1, 5). **Please note** as the number of sts decreases throughout the body, the number of sts you k before your first dot and after your last dot continuously changes.
Beginning with a p row, continue in st st, making a dot or staggered dot row every 10th row (making sure the dots line up in a staggered manner) while at the same time continue decreasing as above until there are 61 (65, 69, 73, 77) sts remaining.
Continue in pattern until piece measures 18 (22, 26, 28, 31)" from cast on edge ending with a p row.

Armhole shaping:
Row 1 (rs): cast off 3 (3, 3, 4, 4) sts, pattern to end.
Row 2 (ws): cast off 3 (3, 3, 4, 4) sts, p to end.
Row 3: cast off 1 st, pattern to end.
Row 4: cast off 1 st, p to end. There are now 53 (57, 61, 63, 67) sts remaining.
Row 5: k1, p1, k1, p1, k1, skp, pattern to last 7 sts, k2tog, k1, p1, k1, p1, k1 (this creates the armhole seed st border).
Row 6: k1, p1, k1, p1, k1, p to last 5 sts, k1, p1, k1, p1, k1.
Repeat rows 5 and 6, 6 (6, 7, 7, 8) more times ending with a p row. There are now 39 (43, 45, 47, 49) sts remaining.

Continue in pattern for 0 (2, 4, 6, 8) rows ending with a p row.

Neck shaping:
Next row (rs): pattern 15 (16, 16, 17, 17) sts, cast off 9 (11, 13, 13, 15) sts, pattern 14 (15, 15, 16, 16) sts. Turn and work on these 15 (16, 16, 17, 17) sts only (right side).
Next row (ws): pattern to end.
Next row: cast off 2 sts, pattern to end.
Next row: pattern to end.
Repeat last two rows 2 (3, 3, 2, 2) more times ending with a ws row.
Next row: cast off 1 (0, 0, 1, 0) st, pattern to end. There are now 7 (7, 7, 9, 10) sts remaining.
Beginning with a p row, continue in pattern until piece measures 24 ½ (29 ½, 34 ½, 37, 41)" from cast on edge. Cast off.

Join in yarn for left side:
Next row (ws): cast off 2 sts, pattern to end.
Next row (rs): pattern to end.
Repeat last two rows 2 (3, 3, 2, 2) more times ending with a rs row.
Next row: cast off 1 (0, 0, 1, 0) st, pattern to end. There are now 7 (7, 7, 9, 10) sts remaining.
Beginning with a k row, continue in pattern until piece measures 24 ½ (29 ½, 34 ½, 37, 41)" from cast on edge. Cast off.

neck edge

Join one shoulder seam. With right side facing, beginning at open shoulder edge, pick up and k107 (123, 135, 151, 163) along entire neck edge.
Row 1: [k1, p1], repeat to last st, k1.
Repeat row 1 four more times.
Cast off.

finishing

Join shoulder and side seams.

notes

Below we have mapped out the first 48 rows in size 2.

1. seed	13. k	25. k, dec (81 sts)	37. k
2. seed	14. p	26. p	38. p
3. seed	15. k, dec (83 sts)	27. k	39. k, staggered dot
4. seed	16. p	28. p	40. p
5. k	17. k	29. k, dot	41. k
6. p	18. p	30. p	42. p
7. k	19. k, staggered dot	31. k	43. k
8. p	20. p	32. p	44. p
9. k, dot	21. k	33. k	45. k, dec (77 sts)
10. p	22. p	34. p	46. p
11. k	23. k	35. k, dec (79 sts)	47. k
12. p	24. p	36. p	48. p

vest

materials	2 (3, 3, 4, 4) balls Brown Sheep Cotton Fleece in Grey Dawn Pair of size US 6 14" knitting needles
gauge	20 sts and 28 rows = 4" square measured over st st using US 6 needles
size	2 (4, 6, 8, 10)
finished measurements	Chest: 28 ½ (30, 32 ½, 34, 36 ½)" Length: 13 ½ (15 ½, 17 ½, 19 ½, 21 ½)"
back	Cast on 71 (75, 81, 85, 91) sts. Row 1 (rs): k. Row 2 (ws): k. Row 3: p1, [k1, p1], repeat to end. Row 4: k1, [p1, k1], repeat to end. These four rows form the pattern. Repeat these four rows until piece measures 9 (10 ½, 12, 13 ½, 15)" from cast on edge ending on row 4. Armhole: Cast off 4 (4, 6, 6, 6) sts at the beginning of next two rows, k to end. There are now 63 (67, 69, 73, 79) sts remaining. Next row: row 3 above. Next row: row 4 above. Repeat rows 1 to 4 until piece measures 13 (15, 17, 19, 21)" from cast on edge. Divide for neck opening (left side): Next row: k20 (22, 22, 23, 25), cast off 23 (23, 25, 27, 29), k to end. Turn and work on these 20 (22, 22, 23, 25) sts only. Work rows 2, 3 and 4 as above. Next row: k. Cast off. Right side neck opening: Join yarn at neck edge and work rows 2, 3 and 4 as above. Next row: k. Cast off.
front	Cast on 71 (75, 81, 85, 91) sts. Row 1 (rs): k. Row 2 (ws): k. Row 3: p1, [k1, p1], repeat to end. Row 4: k1, [p1, k1], repeat to end. These four rows form the pattern. Repeat these four rows until piece measures 9 (10 ½, 12, 13 ½, 15)" from cast on edge ending on row 4.

Armhole:
Cast off 4 (4, 6, 6, 6) sts at the beginning of next two rows, k to end. There are now 63 (67, 69, 73, 79) sts remaining.
Next row: row 3 above.
Next row: row 4 above.
Repeat rows 1 to 4 until piece measures 12 ½ (14 ½, 16, 18, 20)" from cast on edge.

Divide for neck opening (right side):
Next row: k20 (22, 22, 23, 25), cast off 23 (23, 25, 27, 29), k to end. Turn and work on these 20 (22, 22, 23, 25) sts only.
Work rows 2, 3 and 4 as above.
Work rows 1 to 4, 1 (1, 2, 2, 2) more times.
Next row: k.
Cast off.

Left side:
Join yarn at neck edge and work rows 2, 3 and 4 as above.
Work rows 1 to 4, 1 (1, 2, 2, 2) more times.
Next row: k.
Cast off.

finishing   Join side and shoulder seams.

tube top

materials	1 (1, 2, 2, 2) ball(s) Brown Sheep Cotton Fleece in Cotton Ball (See notes below for colors used on pages 24, 31, 32 and back cover) Pair of size US 6 14" knitting needles 1 ½ yards ribbon
gauge	20 sts and 28 rows = 4" square measured over st st using US 6 needles
size	2 (4, 6, 8, 10)
finished measurements	Chest: 18 ½ (20, 21 ½, 23, 25)" Length: 8 ½ (9 ½, 10 ½, 11 ½, 12 ½)"

front & back
alike
	Cast on 46 (50, 54, 58, 62) sts.
	Row 1: [k2, p2], repeat to last 2 sts, k2.
	Row 2: [p2, k2], repeat to last 2 sts, p2.
	Repeat rows 1 and 2 one more time (bottom rib edge).
	Beginning with a k row, continue in st st until piece measures 7 ½ (8 ½, 9 ½, 10 ½, 11 ½)" from cast on edge ending with a p row.
	
	Next row (rs) eyelet row:
	    size 2: [k3, yo, k2tog], repeat to last st, k1.
	    size 4: k2, yo, k2tog, [k3, yo, k2tog], repeat to last st, k1.
	    size 6: k1, [k3, yo, k2tog], repeat to last 3 sts, k3.
	    size 8: k1, [k3, yo, k2tog], repeat to last 2 sts, k2.
	    size 10: [k3, yo, k2tog], repeat to last 2 sts, k2.
	
	Continue for all sizes:
	Next row (ws): p.
	Row 1: [k2, p2], repeat to last 2 sts, k2.
	Row 2: [p2, k2], repeat to last 2 sts, p2.
	Repeat rows 1 and 2 one more time (upper rib edge).
	Cast off in rib.

finishing	Join side seams. Thread ribbon in and out of eyelet row and tie in a bow. For a more secure fit, thread an elastic cord underneath ribbon. Optional: to create shoulder straps, thread ribbon through an eyelet hole in the front and back alike, tying bow at top of shoulder (pictured on page 24 and back cover).
notes	Tube tops photographed on page 24 and back cover are knit in Cotton Ball and tie-dyed in turquoise and hot pink. Tube top photographed on page 31 is knit in Cotton Ball and tie-dyed in hot pink (refer to page 51 for tie-dye instructions). Tube top photographed on page 32 is knit in Mariner Blue.

wrap dress

materials	1 ball Brown Sheep Cotton Fleece in Truffle (A) 3 (3, 4, 5, 6) balls Brown Sheep Cotton Fleece in Dusty Sage (B) Pair of size US 6 14" knitting needles 2 buttons
gauge	20 sts and 28 rows = 4" square measured over st st using US 6 needles
size	2 (4, 6, 8, 10)
finished measurements	Chest: 21 ½ (24, 26 ½, 29, 31)" Length: 19 ½ (22, 25, 30, 33)"
back	Cast on 62 (70, 77, 83, 88) sts with A. K five rows. Join in B, beginning with a k row, continue in st st until piece measures 14 (16, 18, 21, 24)" from cast on edge ending with a p row. Next row (rs): [k5, k2tog], repeat to last 6 (0, 0, 6, 4) sts, k6 (0, 0, 6, 4). There are now 54 (60, 66, 72, 76) sts remaining. Beginning with a p row, continue in st st for three rows ending with a p row.

Armhole shaping:
Next row (rs): join in A, k6 (6, 6, 7, 7), with B k to last 6 (6, 6, 7, 7) sts, join in A, k6 (6, 6, 7, 7) (this creates the contrast color armhole edging).
Next row (ws): with A, k6 (6, 6, 7, 7), with B p to last 6 (6, 6, 7, 7) sts, with A k6 (6, 6, 7, 7).
Repeat last two rows one more time.
Next row (rs): with A, cast off 3 (3, 3, 4, 4) sts, k2, with B k to last 6 (6, 6, 7, 7) sts, with A k6 (6, 6, 7, 7).
Next row (ws): with A, cast off 3 (3, 3, 4, 4) sts, k2, with B p to last 3 sts, with A k3. There are now 48 (54, 60, 64, 68) sts remaining.
Row 1 (dec row): maintaining the contrast armhole edging, k3, skp, k to last 5 sts, k2tog, k3.
Row 2: k3, p to last 3 sts, k3.
Repeat rows 1 and 2 six more times ending with a p row. There are now 34 (40, 46, 50, 54) sts remaining.
Beginning with a k row, continue in st st until armhole measures 4 ½ (5, 6, 7, 8)" ending with a p row.

Divide for neck opening (right side):
Next row (rs): k12 (14, 16, 17, 19). Turn and work on these sts only.
Continue in st st for three rows ending with a p row.
Cast off.

Left side:
Place center 10 (12, 14, 16, 16) sts on holder, rejoin yarn, k12 (14, 16, 17, 19). Turn and work on these sts only.

Continue in st st for three rows ending with a p row.
Cast off.

right front

Cast on 62 (70, 77, 83, 88) sts with A.
K five rows.
Next row (rs): k3, join in B, k to end.
Next row (ws): p to last 3 sts, with A k3 (three st contrast garter edge)
While maintaining the contrast garter edge, continue in st st until piece measures 14 (16, 18, 21, 24)" from cast on edge ending with a p row.
Next row (rs): [k5, k2tog], repeat to last 6 (0, 0, 6, 4) sts, k6 (0, 0, 6, 4).
There are now 54 (60, 66, 72, 76) sts remaining.
Beginning with a p row, continue in st st for three rows ending with a p row.

Armhole and slope shaping:
Row 1 (rs): k3 and leave these sts on holder, with B cast off 2 (2, 2, 4, 4) sts, k to last 6 (6, 6, 7, 7) sts, join in A, k6 (6, 6, 7, 7).
Row 2 (ws): k6 (6, 6, 7, 7), with B p to end.
Row 3: cast off 5 (5, 5, 7, 7) sts, k to last 6 (6, 6, 7, 7) sts, with A k6 (6, 6, 7, 7).
Row 4: k6 (6, 6, 7, 7), with B p to end.
Row 5: cast off 4 (4, 4, 4, 6) sts, k to last 6 (6, 6, 7, 7) sts, with A k6 (6, 6, 7, 7).
Row 6: cast off 3 (3, 3, 4, 4) sts, k2, with B p to end (continue to maintain 3 st contrast garter edge throughout pattern).
Row 7: k2tog, k to last 5 sts, k2tog, k3 (this row decreases one st at slope and armhole edge).
Row 8: k3, p to last 2 sts, p2 tog (this row decreases one st at slope edge).
Row 9: k2tog, k to last 5 sts, k2tog, k3.
Row 10: k3, p to last 2 sts, p2 tog.
Row 11: k2tog, k to last 5 sts, k2tog, k3.
Row 12: k3, p to last 2 sts, p2 tog.
Row 13: k2tog, k to last 5 sts, k2tog, k3.
Row 14: k3, p to last 2 sts, p2 tog.
Row 15: k2tog, k to last 5 sts, k2tog, k3.
Row 16: k3, p to end.
Row 17: k2tog, k to last 5 sts, k2tog, k3.
Row 18: k3, p to end.
Row 19: k2tog, k to last 5 sts, k2tog, k3. There are now 19 (25, 31, 32, 34) sts remaining.
Row 20: k3, p to end.
Row 21: k2tog, k to end.
Repeat rows 20 and 21 until there are 12 (14, 16, 17, 19) sts remaining.
Continue in st st until armhole measures 5 (5 ½, 6 ½, 7 ½, 8 ½)" ending with a p row (you will have worked the same number of rows as for the back). Cast off.

left front

Cast on 62 (70, 77, 83, 88) sts with A.
K five rows.
Next row (rs): join in B, k to last 3 sts, join in A, k3.

Next row (ws): with A k3, with B p to end (three st contrast garter edge). While maintaining the contrast garter edge, continue in st st until piece measures 14 (16, 18, 21, 24)" from cast on edge ending with a p row.
Next row (rs): k6 (0, 0, 6, 4), [k2tog, k5], repeat to end. There are now 54 (60, 66, 72, 76) sts remaining.
Beginning with a p row, continue in st st for three rows ending with a p row.

Armhole and slope shaping:
Row 1 (rs): join in A, k6 (6, 6, 7, 7), with B k to last 3 sts, with A k3.
Row 2 (ws): k3 and leave these sts on holder, with B cast off 2 (2, 2, 4, 4) sts, p to last 6 (6, 6, 7, 7) sts, with A k6 (6, 6, 7, 7).
Row 3: k6 (6, 6, 7, 7), with B k to end.
Row 4: cast off 5 (5, 5, 7, 7) sts, p to last 6 (6, 6, 7, 7) sts, with A k6 (6, 6, 7, 7).
Row 5: k6 (6, 6, 7, 7), with B k to end.
Row 6: cast off 4 (4, 4, 4, 6) sts, with B p to last 6 (6, 6, 7, 7) sts, with A k6 (6, 6, 7, 7).
Row 7: cast off 3 (3, 3, 4, 4) sts, k2, with B skp, k to last 2 sts, k2tog (continue to maintain 3 st contrast garter edge throughout pattern).
Row 8: p2tog, p to last 3 sts, k3 (this row decreases one st at slope edge).
Row 9: k3, skp, k to last 2 sts, k2tog (this row decreases one st at armhole and slope edge).
Row 10: p2tog, p to last 3 sts, k3.
Row 11: k3, skp, k to last 2 sts, k2tog.
Row 12: p2tog, p to last 3 sts, k3.
Row 13: k3, skp, k to last 2 sts, k2tog.
Row 14: p2tog, p to last 3 sts, k3.
Row 15: k3, skp, k to last 2 sts, k2tog.
Row 16: p to last 3 sts, k3.
Row 17: k3, skp, k to last 2 sts, k2tog.
Row 18: p to last 3 sts, k3.
Row 19: k3, skp, k to last 2 sts, k2tog. There are now 19 (25, 31, 32, 34) sts remaining.
Row 20: p to last 3 sts, k3.
Row 21: k to last 2 sts, k2tog.
Repeat rows 20 and 21 until there are 12 (14, 16, 17, 19) sts remaining.
Continue in st st until armhole measures 5 (5 ½, 6 ½, 7 ½, 8 ½)" ending with a p row (you will have worked the same number of rows as for the back). Cast off.

neckband

Join shoulder seams. With right side facing, k3 sts from holder, pick up and k34 (42, 50, 58, 66) sts evenly along front slope to shoulder seam, pick up and k4 sts along back neck slope, k10 (12, 14, 16, 16) sts from holder, pick up and k4 sts along back neck slope, pick up and k34 (42, 50, 58, 66) sts evenly from shoulder and down front slope, k3 sts from holder. There are now 92 (110, 128, 146, 162) sts. K four rows. Cast off.

finishing

Join side seams. Make a loop at end of each neckband. Attach a button to the top of left inside seam and attach second button to the top of right side seam. Left panel will overlap right panel attaching at sides.

heart purse

materials	1 ball Brown Sheep Cotton Fleece in Putty (A) 1 ball Brown Sheep Cotton Fleece in Cherry Moon (B) Pair of size US 6 14" knitting needles
gauge	20 sts and 28 rows = 4" square measured over st st using US 6 needles
finished measurements	6 ½ x 5 ½"
bag	Cast on 31 sts with A. Row 1: k3, [p2, k2], repeat to end. Row 2: [p2, k2], repeat to last 3 sts p3. Repeat rows 1 and 2 one more time. Beginning with a k row, continue in st st until piece measures 6 ½" from cast on edge ending with a p row. Row 1: k15 (A), k1 (B), k15 (A). Row 2: p14 (A), p3 (B), p14 (A). Row 3: k14 (A), k3 (B), k14 (A). Row 4: p13 (A), p5 (B), p13 (A). Row 5: k13 (A), k5 (B), k13 (A). Row 6: p12 (A), p7 (B), p12 (A). Row 7: k12 (A), k7 (B), k12 (A). Row 8: p11 (A), p9 (B), p11 (A). Row 9: k11 (A), k9 (B), k11 (A). Row 10: p10 (A), p11 (B), p10 (A). Row 11: k10 (A), k11 (B), k10 (A). Row 12: p9 (A), p13 (B), p9 (A). Row 13: k9 (A), k13 (B), k9 (A). Row 14: p9 (A), p13 (B), p9 (A). Row 15: k9 (A), k13 (B), k9 (A). Row 16: p9 (A), p6 (B), p1 (A), p6 (B), p9 (A). Row 17: k10 (A), k5 (B), k1 (A), k5 (B), k10 (A). Row 18: p10 (A), p4 (B), p3 (A), p4 (B), p10 (A). Row 19: k11 (A), k3 (B), k3 (A), k3 (B), k11 (A). Row 20: p31 (A). Beginning with a k row, continue in st st until piece measures 10" from cast on edge ending with a p row. Row 1: k3, [p2, k2], repeat to end. Row 2: [p2, k2], repeat to last 3 sts p3. Repeat rows 1 and 2 one more time. Cast off in rib.
finishing	Join side seams. Make an I-cord 11" long (refer to page 51 for I-cord instructions). Attach to upper side seams.

triangle purse

The triangle purse is knit in two pieces. The entire bag can be knit in as little as two hours! Any girl in the world would love to get their hands on one of these.

materials	1 ball Brown Sheep Cotton Fleece in Buttercream (A)
	1 ball Brown Sheep Cotton Fleece in Wisteria (B)
	Pair of size US 6 14" knitting needles
	1 button
gauge	20 sts and 28 rows = 4" square measured over st st using US 6 needles
size	S (L)
finished measurements	Width at bottom of bag: 6 ½ (8)"
	Height: 7 (8 ½)"
flap & back	Both sizes: cast on 3 sts with A.

K two rows.

Next row: k, increasing 1 st at each end (k through front and back of same st).

Next row: k.

Next row (button hole): inc in first st, k1, yo, k2tog, inc in last st. There are now 7 sts.

Next row: k.

Next row: k, increasing 1 st at each end.

Next row: k.

Repeat last two rows 7 (11) more times. There are now 23 (31) sts.

K 13 (15) rows.

Next row: join in B, beginning with a k row, continue in st st for four rows ending with a p row.

Smaller size:
    Row 1 (inc row): k2, m1rs, k to last 2 sts, m1ls, k2.
    Row 2: p.
    Row 3: k.
    Row 4: p.
    Row 5: k.
    Row 6: p.
    Repeat rows 1 to 6 five more times. There are now 35 sts.
    Cast off.

Larger size:
    Row 1 (inc row): k2, m1rs, k to last 2 sts, m1ls, k2.
    Row 2: p.
    Row 3: k.
    Row 4: p.

Row 5: k.
Row 6: p.
Row 7: k.
Row 8: p.
Repeat rows 1 to 8 five more times. There are now 43 sts.
Cast off.

front

Cast on 23 (31) sts with B.
K three rows.
Next row: p.

Smaller size:
Row 1 (inc row): k2, m1rs, k to last 2 sts, m1ls, k2.
Row 2: p.
Row 3: k.
Row 4: p.
Row 5: k.
Row 6: p.
Repeat rows 1 to 6 five more times. There are now 35 sts.
Cast off.

Larger size:
Row 1 (inc row): k2, m1rs, k to last 2 sts, m1ls, k2.
Row 2: p.
Row 3: k.
Row 4: p.
Row 5: k.
Row 6: p.
Row 7: k.
Row 8: p.
Repeat rows 1 to 8 five more times.   There are now 43 sts.
Cast off.

finishing

Join side and bottom seams. Attach button. Make an I-cord 9 ½ (12)" long (refer to page 51 for I-cord instructions). Attach to upper side seams.

leftover throw

This throw is an excellent use for all your leftover Cotton Fleece. It is a fun reminder of all the pieces we knit for this book.

materials	Approximately 900 grams of leftover Brown Sheep Cotton Fleece yarn (or 9 balls of Brown Sheep Cotton Fleece in various colors). Pair of size US 6 14" knitting needles
gauge	20 sts and 28 rows = 4" square measured over st st using US 6 needles
finished measurements	36 x 64"
throw	Cast on 180 sts. K six rows. Next row (rs): join in new color, k. Next row (ws): k5, p to last 5 sts, k5 (this creates a 5 st garter edge on each side). Repeat last two rows changing colors at random intervals (always join in new colors on a rs row) until piece measures 63" from cast on edge ending with a p row. Join in new color, k six rows. Cast off.

seed dress

materials	3 (4, 5, 6, 7) balls Brown Sheep Cotton Fleece in Lime Light Pair of size US 6 14" knitting needles Size 6 crochet hook 1 button
gauge	20 sts and 28 rows = 4" square measured over st st using US 6 needles
size	2 (4, 6, 8, 10)
finished measurements	Chest: 18 (22, 24, 25 ½, 27)" Length: 22 (26, 28, 30, 32)"
back	Cast on 73 (85, 93, 101, 105) sts. Row 1: [k1, p1], repeat to last st, k1. Repeating this row forms the seed sticth pattern. Repeat row 1, 17 more times. Next row (dec row): **keeping seed st correct** (see notes below), dec 1 st at each end (by either k2tog or p2tog). Continue in seed st decreasing 2 sts (as in dec row) every 20th (20th, 18th, 18th, 18th) row until there are 63 (73, 79, 85, 89) sts remaining. Continue in seed st until piece measures 15 (18, 19, 21, 22)" from cast on edge. Next row (dec row): [k2, k2tog], repeat to last 3 (1, 3, 1, 1) st(s), k3 (1, 3, 1, 1). There are now 48 (55, 60, 64, 67) sts remaining. Beginning with a p row, continue in st st until piece measures 17 (20 ½, 22, 24, 25 ½)" from cast on edge ending with a p row. Armhole shaping: Cast off 3 sts at beginning of next two rows. Cast off 2 sts at beginning of next two rows. Cast off 0 (1, 1, 1, 1) st at beginning of next four rows. There are now 38 (41, 46, 50, 53) sts remaining. Beginning with a k row, continue in st st until piece measures 19 (22 ½, 24 ½, 26, 27 ½)" from cast on edge ending with a p row. Divide for opening: Next row (rs): k19 (20, 23, 25, 26). Turn and work on these sts only (right side of back opening). Beginning with a p row, continue in st st until piece measures 22 (26, 28, 30, 32)" from cast on edge ending with a k row. Next row (ws): cast off 9 (10, 11, 13, 12) sts, p to end. There are now 10 (10, 12, 12, 14) sts remaining. Cast off. Left side: Next row (rs): join in yarn, cast off 0 (1, 0, 0, 1), st, k to end. Turn and

work on these 19 (20, 23, 25, 26) sts only.
Beginning with a p row, continue in st st until piece measures 22 (26, 28, 30, 32)" from cast on edge ending with a p row.
Next row (rs): cast off 9 (10, 11, 13, 12) sts, k to end. There are now 10 (10, 12, 12, 14) sts remaining.
Cast off purlwise.

front

Cast on 73 (85, 93, 101, 105) sts.
Row 1: [k1, p1], repeat to last st, k1. Repeating this row forms the seed sticth pattern.
Repeat row 1, 17 more times.
Next row (dec row): **keeping seed st correct** (see notes below), dec 1 st at each end (by either k2tog or p2tog).
Continue in seed st decreasing 2 sts (as in dec row) every 20th (20th, 18th, 18th, 18th) row until there are 63 (73, 79, 85, 89) sts remaining.
Continue in seed st until piece measures 15 (18, 19, 21, 22)" from cast on edge.
Next row (dec row): [k2, k2tog], repeat to last 3 (1, 3, 1, 1) st(s), k3 (1, 3, 1, 1). There are now 48 (55, 60, 64, 67) sts remaining.
Beginning with a p row, continue in st st until piece measures 17 (20 ½, 22, 24, 25 ½)" from cast on edge ending with a p row.

Armhole shaping:
Cast off 3 sts at beginning of next two rows.
Cast off 2 sts at beginning of next two rows.
Cast off 0 (1, 1, 1, 1) st at beginning of next four rows.
There are now 38 (41, 46, 50, 53) sts remaining.
Beginning with a k row, continue in st st until piece measures 20 (24, 26, 28, 30)" from cast on edge ending with a p row.

Neck shaping:
Next row (rs): k15 (16, 18, 20, 21). Turn and work on these sts only (left side of neck opening).
Next row (ws): cast off 2 (2, 2, 3, 3) sts, p to end.
Next row: k.
Next row: cast off 2 (2, 2, 3, 2) sts, p to end.
Next row: k.
Next row: cast off 1 (2, 2, 2, 2) st(s), p to end. There are now 10 (10, 12, 12, 14) sts remaining.
Beginning with a k row, continue in st st until piece measures 22 (26, 28, 30, 32)" from cast on edge ending with a k row.
Next row: p (you will have worked the same number of rows as for the back).
Cast off.

Right side:
Next row (rs): join in yarn, cast off 8 (9, 10, 10, 11) sts, k to end. There are now 15 (16, 18, 20, 21) sts remaining.
Next row: p.
Next row (rs): cast off 2 (2, 2, 3, 3) sts, k to end.

Next row: p.
Next row: cast off 2 (2, 2, 3, 2) sts, k to end.
Next row: p.
Next row: cast off 1 (2, 2, 2, 2) st(s), k to end. There are now 10 (10, 12, 12, 14) sts remaining.
Beginning with a p row, continue in st st until piece measures 22 (26, 28, 30, 32)" from cast on edge ending with a p row.
Next row: k (you will have worked the same number of rows as for the back).
Cast off.

finishing

Join side and shoulder seams. Neck edging: using crochet hook, begin at back opening, single chain crochet to other side continuing for 1" past opening (to make loop for button). Sew loop in place. Attach button. Armhole edging: using crochet hook, begin at side seam and single chain crochet around. Repeat for other armhole.

notes

To keep seed stitch correct, always knit the purl st and purl the knit st.

raglan sweater

materials	1 (1, 1, 2, 2) ball(s) Brown Sheep Cotton Fleece in Truffle (A) 1 (1, 1, 2, 2) ball(s) Brown Sheep Cotton Fleece in Jungle Green (B) 1 ball Brown Sheep Cotton Fleece in Harvest (C) 1 ball Brown Sheep Cotton Fleece in Buttercream (D) Pair of size US 6 14" knitting needles
gauge	20 sts and 28 rows = 4" square measured over st st using US 6 needles
size	2 (4, 6, 8, 10)
finished measurements	Chest: 26 (28, 30, 32, 34)" Length: 15 (16 ½, 18, 20, 23)"
front & back	Cast on 65 (70, 75, 80, 85) sts with A for front (with B for back). Beginning with a k row, continue in st st until piece measures 9 (10, 11, 13, 15)" from cast on edge ending with a p row. Next row (rs): cast off 5 sts, k to end. Next row (ws): cast off 5 sts, p to end. There are now 55 (60, 65, 70, 75) sts remaining. Next row: k3 skp, k to last 5 sts, k2tog, k3. Next row: p. Repeat last two rows until there are 23 (24, 25, 28, 29) sts remaining ending with a p row. Beginning with a k row, continue in st st for eight rows ending with a p row. Cast off.
sleeves	Cast on 40 (41, 44, 44, 43) sts with C for one sleeve (with D for other). Beginning with a k row, continue in st st for eight rows ending with a p row. Next row (inc row): k3, m1ls, k to last 3 sts, m1rs, k3. Beginning with a p row, continue in st st increasing two sts (as in inc row) every 8th row until there are 54 (57, 62, 64, 67) sts, ending with a p row. Continue in st st until piece measures 8 ½ (9 ½, 10 ½, 12 ½, 14 ½)" from cast on edge ending with p row. Next row (rs): cast off 5 sts, k to end. Next row (ws): cast off 5 sts, p to end. There are now 44 (47, 52, 54, 57) sts remaining. Next row: k3, skp, k to last 5 sts, k2tog, k3. Next row: p. Repeat last two rows until there are 12 (11, 12, 12, 11) sts remaining ending with a p row. Beginning with a k row, continue in st st for eight rows ending with a p row. Cast off.
finishing	Join raglan, arm and side seams.
notes	Raglan sweater on title page is knit in Malibu Blue and striped with Nymph.

capris

materials	2 (3, 3, 4, 5) balls Brown Sheep Cotton Fleece in Holly Green (See notes below for color used on page 46) Pair of size US 6 14" knitting needles ⅝" elastic to fit waist
gauge	20 sts and 28 rows = 4" square measured over st st using US 6 needles
size	2 (4, 6, 8, 10)
finished measurements	Waist before elastic is inserted: 26 (29, 32, 34, 37)" Length: 13 ½ (17, 20, 23 ½, 27)"
left & right sides alike	Cast on 79 (86, 93, 100, 107) sts. Row 1: [k1, p1], repeat to last 1 (0, 1, 0, 1) st, k1 (0, 1, 0, 1). Row 2: p1 (0, 1, 0, 1), [k1, p1], repeat to end. Repeat rows 1 and 2 one more time. Next row (rs): k4, p1, [k6, p1], repeat to last 4 sts, k4. Next row (ws): p. Repeat these two rows until piece measures 8 (10, 12, 14, 16)" from cast on edge ending with a p row. Crotch shaping: Next row (rs): cast off 3 sts, p1, [k6, p1], repeat to last 4 sts, k4. Next row (ws): cast off 3 sts, p to end. Next row: k1, skp, pattern to last 3 sts, k2tog, k1. Next row: p. Repeat last two rows three more times ending with a p row. There are now 65 (72, 79, 86, 93) sts remaining. Next row (rs): k4, p1, [k6, p1], repeat to last 4 sts, k4. Next row (ws): p. Repeat last two rows until piece measures 13 ½ (17, 20, 23 ½, 27)" from cast on edge ending with a rs row. Next row (ws): k (this creates the fold over edge). Next row (rs): k4, p1, [k6, p1], repeat to last 4 sts, k4. Next row (ws): p. Repeat last two rows two more times. Cast off.
finishing	Join front, back and inside leg seams. Fold over upper edge and sew in place to form casing leaving a 2" opening. Thread elastic in casing being careful not to twist. Sew elastic to desired size and close casing.
notes	Capris photographed on page 46 are knit in Banana.

color block poncho

The color block poncho is knit in one piece starting at the bottom edge. Each block of color has the same number of rows. When all rows have been worked and the piece is folded in half, the color blocks at the seam will match.

materials	2 balls Brown Sheep Cotton Fleece in Raging Purple (A)
	1 ball Brown Sheep Cotton Fleece in Prairie Lupine (B)
	1 ball Brown Sheep Cotton Fleece in Lilac Haze (C)
	Pair of size US 6 14" knitting needles
gauge	20 sts and 28 rows = 4" square measured over st st using US 6 needles
finished measurements	Width: 16 (18, 20)"
	Length: 17 (21, 26)"
size	Small: 2/4 (Medium: 6/8, Large: 10/12)
poncho	Cast on 81 (91, 101) sts with A.

poncho

Cast on 81 (91, 101) sts with A.
Rows 1 to 6: [k1, p1], repeat to last st, k1 (this forms the seed st border).
Row 7 (rs): k1, p1, k1, p1, k to end (the first 5 sts form the seed st border).
Row 8 (ws): p to last 5 sts, k1, p1, k1, p1, k1.
Repeat last two rows 4 (6, 8) more times ending with a ws row.
Join in B and repeat rows 7 and 8 above 8 (10, 12) times.
Join in A and repeat rows 7 and 8 above 8 (10, 12) times.
Join in C and repeat rows 7 and 8 above 8 (10, 12) times.
Join in A and repeat rows 7 and 8 above 8 (10, 12) times.
Join in B and repeat rows 7 and 8 above 8 (10, 12) times.
Join in A and repeat rows 7 and 8 above 8 (10, 12) times.
Join in C and repeat rows 7 and 8 above 8 (10, 12) times.
Join in A and repeat rows 7 and 8 above 8 (10, 12) times.
Join in B and repeat rows 7 and 8 above 8 (10, 12) times.
Join in A and repeat rows 7 and 8 above 8 (10, 12) times.
Join in C and repeat rows 7 and 8 above 8 (10, 12) times.
Join in A and repeat rows 7 and 8 above 8 (10, 12) times.
Join in B and repeat rows 7 and 8 above 8 (10, 12) times.
Join in A and repeat rows 7 and 8 above 5 (7, 9) times.
Next six rows: [k1, p1], repeat to last st, k1.
Cast off in pattern.

finishing

Fold poncho in half. Beginning at cast on edge of the stockinette side, join side seam leaving a 7 (9, 11)" neck opening.

gift bag

Make any gift even more special with this packaging. The lucky recipient can use the gift bag as a shoulder bag by tying the ribbon at the ends.

materials	1 ball Brown Sheep Cotton Fleece in Tea Rose (A) 1 ball Brown Sheep Cotton Fleece in Wisteria (B) Pair of size US 6 14" knitting needles 2 lengths of ribbon each 36"
gauge	20 sts and 28 rows = 4" square measured over st st using US 6 needles
finished measurements	11 ½ x 11"
back	Cast on 58 sts with A. Beginning with a k row, continue in st st for six rows ending with a p row. Next two rows: k (this creates the fold over edge at the top of bag). Beginning with a k row, continue in st st for four rows ending with a p row. Next row (hole row): join in B, k3, yo, k2tog, k to last 5 sts, k2tog, yo, k3. Next row: p. Beginning with a k row, continue in st st for 70 rows ending with a p row. Cast off.
front	Cast on 58 sts with A. Beginning with a k row, continue in st st for six rows ending with a p row. Next two rows: k (this creates the fold over edge at the top of bag). Beginning with a k row, continue in st st for four rows ending with a p row. Next row (hole row): join in B, k3, yo, k2tog, k to last 5 sts, k2tog, yo, k3. Beginning with a p row, continue in st st for three rows ending with a p row. Join in A, continue in st st for four rows ending with a p row. Join in B, continue in st st for four rows ending with a p row. Continue in st st alternating colors every four rows for 60 rows (you will have worked the same number of rows as for the back). Cast off.
finishing	Join side and bottom seams. Fold over upper edge and sew in place to form casing. Beginning on one side, thread ribbon through entire casing exiting on same side. Repeat for other side.

button pillows

The whimsical nature of these pillows makes them a great addition to any room. Instead of the heart or flower button pattern, monogram a single initial out of buttons.

materials	For heart: 1 ball Brown Sheep Cotton Fleece in Putty (A) 1 ball Brown Sheep Cotton Fleece in Cherry Moon (B) 1 ball Brown Sheep Cotton Fleece in Wild Orange (C) For flower pillow: 1 ball Brown Sheep Cotton Fleece in Putty (A) 1 ball Brown Sheep Cotton Fleece in Wisteria (D) 1 ball Brown Sheep Cotton Fleece in Buttercream (E) 1 ball Brown Sheep Cotton Fleece in Nymph (F) 1 ball Brown Sheep Cotton Fleece in Wild Orange (G) Pair of size US 6 14" knitting needles 14" down pillow insert Buttons for decoration
gauge	20 sts and 28 rows = 4" square measured over st st using US 6 needles
finished measurements	14 x 14"
front (heart & flower)	Cast on 70 sts with A. Beginning with a k row, continue in st st until piece measures 14" from cast on edge ending with a p row. Cast off.
back (heart)	Cast on 70 sts with B. Beginning with a k row, continue in st st alternating colors B and C every two rows until piece measures 14" from cast on edge ending with p row. Cast off.
back (flower)	Cast on 70 sts with D. Beginning with a k row, continue in st st alternating colors D, E, F and G every two rows until piece measures 14" from cast on edge ending with p row. Cast off.
finishing	Join side and bottom seams. Insert pillow form and join top seam. Arrange buttons in a heart or three flower pattern and sew in place.

resources

Brown Sheep Company, Inc.
100662 County Road 16
Mitchell, Nebraska 69357
brownsheep.com

Lantern Moon
7911 NE 33rd Drive Suite 140
Portland, Oregon 97211
lanternmoon.com
Lantern Moon produces knitting needles handmade from the finest hardwoods available. They work directly with producers to provide income, education and self-reliance to Vietnamese women and their families.

Hanah Silk™
Bias-cut hand-dyed silk ribbons (photographed on pages 15, 24, 28, 31, 32 and 44)

Dylon® Permanent Fabric Dye
available at Hancock Fabrics

The Knitter's Companion, Vicki Square
Interweave Press, 1996
for instructions on m1rs and m1ls

acknowledgements

our special thanks to

Chuck Coon of Toof Press (Memphis, TN) for guiding us through the publishing process.

Judy Wilson of Brown Sheep Company (Mitchell, NE) for her advice.

Antje Loeffler for entertaining and loving our children.

Tammy, Mary, Ritu, Mary, Kathy, Tammy and Mai for fitting us into their schedules so willingly.

Chris and Missy for inspiring us to write our first pattern.

Dana, Myrna, Jacky, Elisa, Sue, Susan and Eileen for not only lending an ear, but also giving great advice.

A special thank you to our models who always wore a smile.

Finally, thank you to our families for their insight and support, especially our husbands and children without whom, we would have never been inspired to write this book.